SOURCES AND SHAPES
OF POWER

D1474973

Into Our Third Century Series

The Church in a Changing Society, William E. Ramsden
Images of the Future, Alan K. Waltz
In Praise of Learning, Donald B. Rogers
Women, Change, and the Church, Nancy J. Van Scoyoc
Shaping the Congregation, Robert L. Wilson
Ministries Through Non-Parish Institutions, William E. Ramsden
Sources and Shapes of Power,
    John R. Sherwood and John C. Wagner

SOURCES
AND SHAPES
OF POWER

JOHN R. SHERWOOD
and
JOHN C. WAGNER

Ezra Earl Jones, Editor

ABINGDON   Nashville

SOURCES AND SHAPES OF POWER

Library of Congress Cataloging in Publication Data

SHERWOOD, JOHN R 1924–
  Sources and shapes of power.
  (Into our third century)
  1. United Methodist Church (United States)—Government.
  I. Wagner, John C., 1931– joint author. II. Jones, Ezra Earl.
  III. Title.
  BX8382.2.S53   262'.07673   80-28125

ISBN 0-687-39142-3

MANUFACTURED BY THE PARTHENON PRESS AT
NASHVILLE, TENNESSEE, UNITED STATES OF AMERICA

Contents

Foreword

The United Methodist Church is a multilevel organization of church members, congregations, districts, conferences, jurisdictional or central conferences, and general church structures. At each level the church strives to be faithful by performing the responsibilities assigned to it. There are, at each level, followers and leaders—members, delegates, and appointed or elected staff.

Structurally, the basic unit of The United Methodist organization is the Annual Conference. It is at this level that administrative leadership is most visible and that decisions are made which have immediate effect upon persons and groups at all other levels. Essentially, The United Methodist Church is "a federation of Annual Conferences." The Annual Conference supervises the recruitment and training of the clergy; elects delegates to jurisdictional and general conferences; and establishes appropriate formulas for apportioning financial responsibility to the congregations for support of the church's ministry around the world. The bishops, each resident in an area of at least one Annual Conference, are the chief executive officers of the denomination. A bishop assigns the clergy to lead the respective congregations in an Annual Conference—a task that is done annually. The district superintendents and conference staff also are conference officers and leaders.

It is appropriate, then, that a study of leadership and administration in The United Methodist Church would center on the Annual Conference. While they interviewed members and leaders at several levels of the church, Sherwood and Wagner focused their attention on the dynamics of current leadership patterns in the Annual Conferences and their effects on the total ministry of the denomination. In sample conferences in each jurisdiction, the authors talked to a great many people about conditions that affect the ability of leaders to lead and the willingness of the church to follow. They went back to the sources of leadership and adminstrative authority in the early church and in early United Methodism, to provide a framework in which the present patterns of management may be examined and evaluated. They developed and explored hypotheses concerning problems and possibilities, and now in this book, they offer specific recommendations to The United Methodist Church as it moves into its third century.

We in the General Council on Ministries invite you to travel with the authors on a brief journey through the maze of administrative corridors which United Methodists have developed over these 200 years. It is not a long trip, but it will acquaint you with the complexities of managing a 9.6-million member, worldwide, not for profit, volunteer organization. We believe the insights shared here can help all United Methodists become better leaders or better followers, or both. When you have read this book, share your reflections within your own congregation, with other Christians, and with district, conference, and general church leaders. Write to us at the General Council on Ministries or write to the authors themselves. They have begun the process of identifying the problems. As we all reflect on these problems and seek new directions, our church can move toward renewed life and ministry.

This book is the seventh volume in the United Methodist Into Our Third Century series. In 1984, United Methodism will observe the 200th anniversary of the Christmas Conference of 1784—the date most often regarded as the beginning of the Methodist movement in the United States. Our bicentennial is a time to anticipate the future soberly and to take stock of ourselves and our life together as we move into the third century. Some indicators of our future prospects are disturbing; this is a time for us to reflect on and to discuss these concerns. By doing so, perhaps we will catch a vision, once again, of ministry and service that is worthy of our past, builds upon our present, and thrusts us into the future with the message of God's redeeming love.

The Into Our Third Century series, initiated by the General Council on Ministries, with the encouragement of the Council of Bishops and the General Council on Finance and Administration, is intended to support that reflection and discussion. It is an extensive study of selected issues of fundamental ministerial and organizational concern to the denomination and also a study of the environment in which United Methodism serves. Over a four-year period, beginning in 1980 and concluding in our bicentennial year, eighteen separate volumes dealing with the present realities and future challenges of our denomination and our ministry are being released.

It is our hope in the General Council on Ministries that you, the United Methodist lay leaders, pastors, and congregations, will have vital roles in both the celebration and the look ahead. It is the people in the pews and pulpits of United Methodism who must reestablish our identity and purpose for the next century. It is our belief and hope that this volume will contribute to that goal.

Norman E. Dewire
General Secretary

Ezra Earl Jones
Editor

General Council on Ministries
601 West Riverview Avenue
Dayton, Ohio 45406

April, 1981

CHAPTER 1

Introduction

Our assignment has been to explore the nature of leadership and administration in The United Methodist Church. The purpose of this book is to share what we have found and to propose directions for the future.

We have our own experiences, ways of thinking, learning, and opinions, and so it is only fair that we share with you a little of this "baggage" we bring to the task.

As John Sherwood, I am an Episcopal layman, with experience as layreader-in-charge of a small congregation and, for thirteen years, as the executive layman of the Diocese of Southern Ohio. For the past eleven years, I have been consultant to a variety of churches, conferences, assemblies, and institutions.

As John Wagner, I am a United Methodist clergyman, with many years of experience as pastor, conference staff member, congregational consultant, and seminary teacher. At present, I am a professor of church administration at the United Theological Seminary in Dayton, Ohio.

We see leadership and administration as two related faces of governance in the life of the church. They require separate, very different activities, but they are like the two sides of a coin: They are integral to each other—we cannot have one without the other.

Leadership has been defined as the responsible exercise of power. Some people become concerned when we talk about power, and it is important that we share some of our assumptions:

—Power comes from God.

—The people of God are empowered through the action of the Holy Spirit.

—The people of God, in turn, empower their leaders and administrators.

—As the Church remains faithful, it is guided by the Holy Spirit.

Leadership in the church includes presiding over the rituals that empower the people of God. Specifically, these rituals take three broad forms:

—Recall the heritage of the church—tell the stories of salvation that reveal the gospel and the particular identity of The United Methodist Church;

—Hold before the people the vision and mission of the church;

—Call forth their hopes and dreams and shape these into clear intentions. Out of these intentions comes a commitment—a stance, a mobilization and focusing of energies ("we will"), a covenanting of the people, individually and collectively, to fulfill Christ's mission and ministry in the world.

Administration is the enactment of those intentions, carrying out the tasks of ministry that bring the intentions to life. It is the responsibility of administration to:

—Delegate the tasks of ministry to specific people, specific groups;

—Authorize those people to act and support them with resources to get the job done;

—Provide authentic evaluation, which honors people for real achievements, improves the quality of ongoing ministry, shares with the whole church what has been learned from the experience, and builds new possibilities for the future.

The subject is broad and inclusive of many aspects of church life. In order to provide both a deeper comprehension and practical help, we chose the Annual Conference as a major focus for our study. The conference has been a powerful agent in the history of The United Methodist Church. We believe that the issues facing leadership and administration in the Annual Conference are similar to those confronting the denomination as a whole, including the local churches.

Design for Exploration

Our search for models and principles for the future of church leadership and administration begins with origins. In the first section of this book, we will seek to enter the life of the early church—the way the gospel was expressed by the first generations of Christ's followers. As we discover the earliest roots of church life, we also may find clues to the understanding of our current experience and our directions for the future. We move next to search out the sources of The United Methodist Church in those strategic events that resulted in the formation of the Methodist, Evangelical, and United Brethren denominations. As movements for renewal took on structure and enduring forms of governance, the foundations of our current experience were laid. The first section closes with a summary of the instructions in *The Book of Discipline of The United Methodist Church, 1980* (referred to hereafter as *The Discipline*) regarding the Annual Conference and its leadership and administration.

The second section relates what we have seen and heard in Annual Conferences across the United States. We touched only a portion of the denomination, but what we found was illuminating, and we would like to share it with you. We visited Annual Conferences when they were in session. We listened to lay people, pastors, district superintendents, and bishops, as they participated in and as they described their experience of leadership and administration in the Annual Conference. Almost one thousand laity and clergy responded to a survey regarding issues that affect the character of church governance. The results of that survey are summarized and some hypotheses are made.

The last portion of the book identifies some strategic questions that have emerged from our study and research, and it proposes a model, or direction for the future.

Acknowledgments

We would like to express our appreciation to our editor, Ezra Earl Jones; the faculty and staff of United Theological Seminary and of Management Design, Inc.; the General Council on Ministries; and the Annual Conferences that were involved in our study and analysis. Our thanks go also to Princeton, Drew, and Wesley seminaries, and to the College of Preachers, for their assistance and facilities for research and writing. We are grateful, as well, to Miriam Wagner and Shirley Sherwood for their contributions.

John R. Sherwood
John C. Wagner

CHAPTER 2

The Origins of Leadership and Administration in the Early Church

Church renewal and reformation have been associated with the rediscovery and reappropriation of the Scriptures. In the midst of crises and in ordinary daily existence, Christians bear witness to the transforming power of God encountered in Scripture. *The Discipline* of The United Methodist Church reflects the understanding of the primacy of Scripture in any consideration of Christian faith and life.

> United Methodists share with all other Christians the conviction that Scripture is the primary source and guideline for doctrine. The Bible is the deposit of a unique testimony to God's self-disclosures: in the world's creation, redemption and final fulfillment; in Jesus Christ as the incarnation of God's Word; in the Holy Spirit's constant activity in the dramas of history. It is the primitive source of the memories, images, and hopes by which the Christian community came into existence and that still confirm and nourish its faith and understanding. (Par. 69)

The purpose of this chapter is to explore the emerging patterns of leadership as they are expressed in the New Testament materials, and also in several later writings of the first and second centuries, as the Christian movement took on sustained institutional forms. The objective is not only to describe a process, but to discern the witness of the church to its Lord and to allow the Spirit to illumine our way, as we seek to understand our current experience and to propose a model for leadership and administration.

The New Testament reveals the development of Christian

communities centered originally around Jesus of Nazareth—communities of faith that bore witness to the life, teachings, death, and resurrection of their Lord and the Savior of the world. The purpose, power, unity, and diversity of the early church all found their source in the Christ whose coming they proclaimed, and who stands at the center of any meaningful understanding of church leadership and administration.

Hans von Campenhausen provides one key to understanding the development of church order, when he speaks of the relationship of Word and Spirit, tradition and gift. When we look at the early church, we always find some relationship between the office (elder, deacon, bishop, etc.) and the gifts of the Holy Spirit. "The crucial factor is the firm correlation in which from the very first the 'Spirit' stands to the concept of the 'Word' or 'testimony,' both of which go back to the person of Jesus himself."[1] The Word—the tradition of the gospel—is not the same as the Holy Spirit, but must be brought into proper relationship with the experience of the presence of God. To exclude Word/tradition is to risk emotional distortions of the faith. To exclude Spirit/gift is to risk authoritarian distortions of church order. The power of the early church was due in some measure to the way that Word and Spirit, tradition and gift, were intimately and effectively related to one another in the living experience of the earliest Christian communities.

As we look at the Gentile churches of Paul's correspondence and at the Acts of the Apostles, we find a common allegiance to Christ and a diversity in corporate life, leadership, and administration which provided the ground for later developments of church governance. Our purpose is not to call for slavish imitation of early forms of church organization. Clearly, leadership and administration in the first centuries of the Christian era were exercised in quite different situations from our own. But we are convinced that the initial experience of the churches as they formed their corporate life may illumine our way as we seek to understand the enduring issues, problems, and possibilities of church order.

Von Campenhausen describes the historic paradox of tradition and Spirit—apparently opposed realities of corporate life in the church, but fundamentally related. The following chart, adapted from his book, illustrates the tension between office and spiritual gift, which found expression in differences between the Christianity of Paul and that initially established in Jerusalem. Subsequent generations expressed those differences and sought to maintain the connection between tradition and Spirit, but office gradually assumed a primary role as the church became an established institution. The remainder of this chapter explores the development of leadership and administration in the light of that "historic paradox."

THE HISTORIC PARADOX[2]

Tradition	--------------------	Spirit
Office	--------------------	Spiritual Gift

United in
Jesus' authority
in himself

In the Apostles'
authority in the encounter with
the risen Lord

authoritarian distortion	"enthusiast" distortion
Palestinian Christianity	*Pauline Christianity*
Led by presbyter/elders, with official authority based on position, age, personal influence, experience. The moral importance and effectiveness of human attributes enhance the church. Offices are spiritual in	Emphasized the sovereignty of the Spirit, demonstrated in human weakness. Christians are free to reject human authority but are called to mutual submission of those endowed by the Spirit. This "charismatic

terms of origin and goals, as well as in the manner of fulfillment. Faithful maintenance of the tradition is crucial if the power of God is to be demonstrated.

constitution of the church" understands functions and ministries as spiritual gifts, broadly distributed by the Spirit. There is no office apart from such gifts.

Fusion of Palestinian and Pauline Christianity

The Pastoral Epistles demonstrate regard for elders and for spiritual gifts. As a historic communion, the church is committed to preservation of the integrity and continuity of tradition. Offices have a spiritual commission to preach, teach, worship, and maintain discipline—not as an absolute right, but in relationship with the spiritual community as a whole and with its spiritual gifts. The function of office is to point to the living Lord. The question is, How true to the Master and to the meaning of commission are the congregation and its office holders, in the exercise of their responsibilities?

Gradual Ascendancy of Office in the Early Church

A shift to the preponderance of the official elements of the church was reflected in the writings of the Apostolic Fathers. Faced with divisive sects claiming the Spirit and with threats to links with the history of the church and to the historicity of Jesus, official safeguards were reestablished to maintain the integrity of the church. The authority of councils of elders and bishops was understood as being derived from Christ. The hierarchy was accepted, and the monoepiscopate (rule by one bishop) appears.

The Church of Paul

Paul used the term "gifts" to describe the varied capabilities, ministries, and functions that arose within the Gentile Christian communities, and his letters to the Corinthians reflect his understanding that Christ was the source of those gifts.

I give thanks to God always for you because of the grace of God which was given you in Christ Jesus, that in every way you were enriched in him with all speech and all knowledge—even as the testimony to Christ was confirmed among you—so that you are

not lacking in any spiritual gift, as you wait for the revealing of our
Lord Jesus Christ; who will sustain you to the end, guiltless in the
day of our Lord Jesus Christ. God is faithful, by whom you were
called into the fellowship of his Son, Jesus Christ our Lord. (I Cor.
1:4-9)

For Paul, the central reality was the grace of God, freely given
in Christ, which grants every spiritual gift to all those who call
on the Lord. The source of all our gifts is Christ, and our
appropriation of those gifts is made possible only by the
invitation to be part of his fellowship.

The image Paul conveys is of a church in which the gifts of
the Spirit are broadly distributed among Christ's followers. It
was a community of faith, hope, and love, for whom Christ
was central and the proclamation of the gospel the overriding
concern.

Paul understood his authority as coming not from his own
weak and fearful human powers, but from faithful proclamation of the cross of Christ—the power of the gospel came
from the power of God.

He was convinced, moreover, that the authority of the
church as a whole lay not in its status or sophistication, but in
its life in Christ.

For consider your call, brethren; not many of you were wise
according to worldly standards, not many were powerful, not
many were of noble birth; but God chose what is foolish in the
world to shame the wise, God chose what is weak in the world to
shame the strong, God chose what is low and despised in the
world, even things that are not, to bring to nothing things that are,
so that no human being might boast in the presence of God. He is
the source of your life in Christ Jesus, whom God made our
wisdom, our righteousness and sanctification and redemption;
therefore, as it is written, "Let him who boasts, boast of the Lord."
(I Cor. 1:26-31)

Paul challenged the conventional view, which saw power as
derived from knowledge, wealth, status, or prestige. On the
contrary, he maintained that God chose the powerless to

demonstrate the power of the Spirit, so that faith should rest not in human invention, but in Christ, the source of eternal life. The purpose of the church lies not in building a human enterprise, but in continuing the ministry and mission of Christ in the world. For that task, only the power of God is sufficient.

Paul, writing to a diverse and often fragmented congregation in Corinth, expressed his understanding of the gifts of the Spirit and the source of their unity in Christ. He used the familiar analogy of the mutual interdependence of the parts of the body, maintaining that even those parts that seem weaker or less honorable are, in fact, indispensable. Such God-given unity and diversity has been called the charismatic constitution of the Church. Grounded in Jesus Christ, expressed in the gifts of the Spirit, the Church serves a common Lord through a mutual ministry.

Paul lists a variety of gifts: the utterance of Godly wisdom and knowledge, faith, healing, the working of miracles, prophecy, the ability to distinguish between spirits, to speak in tongues, and to interpret tongues.[3] In a subsequent passage, he adds certain roles to the list. "Now you are the body of Christ and individually members of it. And God has appointed in the church first apostles, second prophets, third teachers, then workers of miracles, then healers, helpers, administrators, speakers in various kinds of tongues" (I Cor. 12:27-28). The vital connection between tradition and Spirit is demonstrated in the priority Paul assigns to apostles, prophets, and teachers. The apostles were those who had been called by the historic Jesus and who, after his death and resurrection, proclaimed what they had seen and heard. The prophets were probably itinerant preachers who traveled among the churches, demonstrating divine power in words and deeds. The teachers presumably were divinely inspired interpreters of the Christian tradition, who called people to ethical conduct.[4] Paul's inclusion of prophets and teachers affirms their charismatic (Spirit-filled) activity, not over against tradition, but in immediate relation to the original testimony in which Word and Spirit were clearly joined.

The helpers and administrators to whom Paul refers probably were people such as those who were "over" the church in Thessalonica. After his direction to encourage one another, he charges the members "to respect those who labor among you and are over you in the Lord and admonish you, and to esteem them very highly in love because of their work. Be at peace among yourselves" (I Thess. 5:12-13). Carrying out Paul's appeal that things be done "decently and in order" (I Cor. 14:40) may be understood as being not the responsibility solely of leaders and administrators, but of the community as a whole. Calling on Christians to be united in the Spirit, he urges them to demonstrate, through self-giving love, "the more excellent way," as described in the thirteenth chapter of I Corinthians.

It was later that the activities of helping and administering were expressed in offices or in official responsibilities. In Philippians, one of Paul's later letters, the greeting is, "To all the saints in Christ Jesus who are at Philippi, with the bishops and deacons" (1:1*b*). The Greek term for bishop, *episkopos,* is used only five times in the New Testament and only once in Paul's letters. In his letter to the Philippians, Paul speaks of their "bishops," referring to a number of people in the same congregation who filled an important but unspecified office.

Paul's use of the term "deacon" in Philippians is probably the oldest reference to that office in the New Testament indicating some kind of identifiable and continuing ministry in the community by persons associated with bishops. In Pauline communities, deacons were responsible for caring for the needy and "attending to material things."[5]

The roles of bishops and deacons were recognizable; however, in Paul's letters they could not be viewed as holy offices, but as ministries that arose as needed within the life of the congregation.

> The gift of the Spirit which is the basis of each ministry within the congregation cannot be "handed on," but in every instance is directly bestowed by the Spirit himself.

The tension, fundamental to any office, namely between personal capacity and the duties imposed, is therefore lacking. In this contact, to pursue a "calling" is simply to exercise, to confirm, to prove a particular gift which has been received; and it is the presence of this gift that demonstrates a true "call," and makes its implementation possible.

Paul knows of no "obedience," in the strict sense of the word, toward those in authority within the congregation such as he demands toward Christ and therefore, in principle, toward Christ's apostle.[6]

Paul's understanding of his own authority was derived from the direct apostolic commission he received from the risen Christ, in which he might properly command the congregations for whom he felt responsibility. But rarely did he command, preferring for the sake of the gospel to appeal for freely chosen and responsible behavior. "For the person in authority within the congregation there is still only the life of humility, of mutual subordination of every member, and of spontaneity as great in serving as in obeying."[7]

For Paul, the character of church life is bound up in the gracious self-giving of Christ, through whom we become members of his Body, empowered to proclaim the cross and resurrection and to serve in his Spirit. Paul's letters contain no clearer conception of the relationship of faith and order than in the "servant" passage found in Philippians (2:1-11).

Word and Spirit, tradition and gift, are integrally related for Paul and are expressed in his conviction that it is Christ who is Lord of the church and that it is the gifts of his Spirit that empower the community of faith. It is in Christ that the activities, functions, and emerging roles find their power and unity. It is in self-giving service that the church expresses its relationship to the crucified and risen Lord.

The Church in Jerusalem

In his Gospel, Luke had recorded the coming of Jesus of Nazareth—the fulfillment of the Law and the Prophets—the crucifixion, and the resurrection. In The Acts of the Apostles, he tells of the formation of the Christian community, the New Israel, an apostolic fellowship empowered by the Holy Spirit to proclaim the good news of God's saving action in Jesus Christ. In the Gospel of Luke and in Acts, Jerusalem was the center, the focus, not only for the climactic events of Jesus' life, but for the founding of the early church as well.

The Christian community, the New Israel, was required to identify with and also to distinguish itself from the Judaism into which it was born. The first disciples were Jews, inheriting the thought-forms and structures of Judaism and understanding themselves within the faith and life of Israel. But with Jesus' death and resurrection, the earliest Christians found themselves to be a community of a "third order," different from both the Jews for whom the Messiah had not yet appeared and the Gentiles who did not confess him as Lord. Acts tells the story of the early church from the perspective of Jerusalem and the Christianity of Palestine.

The book of Acts is a testimony to God's providential care. The speeches of Peter and the others bear witness to God's saving action in and through the Christian communities. Defeats are turned into triumphs by the power of the Holy Spirit. God is dependable and ultimately undefeatable. The church is the agent of a gospel that cannot be overcome by opposition or even by persecution. As God upheld the prophets, so he raised Jesus from the dead, and by his mighty acts he vindicates the apostles who proclaim the good news to Jews and Gentiles. The continuity of the church is assured.

Luke empowers the church by retelling the stories of Jesus and the apostles—maintaining connections with the dramatic events that lie at the heart of the gospel the early church proclaims. The identity of the church is confirmed.

The issues of identity and continuity are addressed in Acts not only by the words of the apostles, but by the way the Christian community was organized. In Acts 1, Luke tells of the selection and enrollment of Matthias as one of the Twelve, to maintain the number after Judas had betrayed the

Lord and died. In chapter 6, we read of the appointment of "seven men of good repute" to serve tables, freeing the apostles for the important work of preaching the gospel. These seven were "set before the apostles, and they prayed and laid their hands upon them" (6:6).

The narrative concerning the laying on of hands confirms Luke's emphasis not only on preaching but on the maintenance of the Christian community. Although the passage does not use the word "deacon," it does provide grounds for understanding the origin of that office and its holders' responsibility for the temporal welfare of the church.

With continuity and providential care as major themes, it is not surprising to find "elders" playing a major role in Palestinian Christianity. "Elders" may be understood as referring either to persons of advanced age or to those who hold supervisory offices, or both. The first use of the term that denotes their official function is found in Acts 11:30, when Paul and Barnabas bring to the elders in Jerusalem the collection gathered to meet the needs of the saints in that "mother church." The elders' role is visible again at the council in Jerusalem, which met to deal with the matter of the observance of Jewish law by Gentile Christians.

Later in Acts, the elders emerge as an official body, with James serving as a major figure among them. With the death of the apostles, the office of elder took on increasing importance by providing respected persons to maintain the identity, continuity, and integrity of the faith. It was necessary for someone to maintain the crucial memories, the tradition, the content of the gospel. They needed someone to be responsible for the good order of the church. It was to the elders that the major responsibility for faith and order was assigned.

The book of Acts records the emergence of Palestinian Christianity, which differed from the church order of Pauline communities, but Hans Küng warns against construing them simply as opposites. The "system of elders" later may have degenerated into church bureaucracy, but at its beginning it was far from that. The Pauline "charismatic constitution" of the church later may have broken down into conflicting sectarianism, but Paul stood firmly against such disorder. Both Pauline and Palestinian Christianity presupposed the witness of the original apostles. Both affirmed faith in the gospel and in baptism. Both discerned the origin of ministries to be in the call of God, and they affirmed the church's responsibility to confirm or reject any claim of divine call.[8]

From the very beginning, people were different in their responses to Jesus, and the development of the early church reflects the rich diversity of Christian faith and the variety of communities through which it was expressed. With differing emphasis, both Pauline and Palestinian conceptions of church order reflected the interdependence of Word and Spirit, office and gift.

Timothy and Titus

The letters to Timothy and Titus are part of a later correspondence in the New Testament, clustered under the title Pastoral Letters. Titus and First and Second Timothy were addressed to Christians who were aware of the lengthening history of the church and of its distinctive role in society. In those letters we find Paul providing, through particular offices, not only for the church of his own and the next generation, but for subsequent generations as well.

In the midst of a hostile and changing world, the early church was concerned with stabilization of its internal life. That stability was sought through sound teaching by reliable persons who were authorized to speak to and for the community of faith.

In the letters to Timothy and Titus, church order is established by the transmission of authority through the laying on of hands. That act served to maintain the continuity of church leadership and administration. It was not simply a matter of human initiative, but the mediation, through the laying on of hands, of the gift of God, made known through the prophets. But a crucial shift is taking place. From gifts immediately given by the Spirit, apart from human initiative, the letters to Timothy bear witness to certain gifts that were received when elders laid their hands upon persons selected for positions of authority.

The development of faith and order in the early church is apparent in both Timothy and Titus. The effort to deal with internal and external challenges is clear and understandable. Offices were established to provide for sound teaching and holy living. But there were dangers embedded in the process as well; Eduard Schweizer identifies some of those issues: "Is not the sequence threatened with inversion so that it is no longer the case that one who is called by God receives through the Church the opportunity of carrying out his commission, but rather the one who is appointed to a ministry is thereby guaranteed the acquisition of the divine gift for it?"[9] Schweizer goes on to point out the problem of a church that is content merely to repeat an old message, but fails to experience God's living Spirit. Although the church of the Pastorals may not have succumbed to such perils, the community of faith continued to move in those directions, and subsequent generations of Christians were destined to struggle with the dangers of legalistic and lifeless church order.

The Church of the Apostolic Fathers

The earliest Christian writings after the New Testament were those of the Apostolic Fathers. Included in this group are materials that reflect crucial developments in church order, beyond but related to New Testament conceptions. Although these writings do not serve the primary role of Scripture, they do show us something of the consequences of New Testament Christianity and the emerging shape of leadership and administration in generations to come. In fact, there is reason to claim that in the church order of the

Fathers, we can see the shape of major developments in church order for many generations—for our time, as well. We will be looking at *The First Letter of Clement,* the *Didache,* and the letters of Ignatius of Antioch, as examples of that crucial period in the life of the church.

The First Letter of Clement, probably written in A.D. 96, from the church of Rome to the church of Corinth, was occasioned by a schism or split in the congregation.

It was not unusual for the leaders of one congregation to send letters of advice and warning to another. Local churches were independent but not isolated units in the wider church, as both New Testament and other Christian writings show. Accordingly, Clement, a bishop in the Roman church, sent to Corinth the letter known as *I Clement.*

He calls for the repentance of those involved in the "abominable and unholy schism," and for humility, adherence to peace, and obedient submissiveness (19:1). Reverence for Christ and fear of God require respect for the church's ruling elders. Another crucial transition in church order is reflected in this identification of faith with obedience.

Clement does summon the leaders and administrators to care for the weak and the poor, but that does not lessen his insistence on respect for church order. The weak should look up to the strong, and the poor should thank God for giving them someone to meet their needs.

Clement views the origin of the elders' authority in apostolic terms. Indeed, there still were members of the church who had known the original apostles, and who in their lifetime had seen the inauguration of offices.

His description of "the orderly procedure" (42:1-4) roots the current church order firmly in the providence of God, through Christ and the apostles. It is clear that for Clement, church order was according to divine plan and was reflected in the experience of the church. In fact, he claims the apostles had foreknowledge of the conflict.

> Now our apostles, thanks to our Lord Jesus Christ, knew that there was going to be strife over the title of bishop. It was for this reason and because they had been given an accurate knowledge of the future, that they appointed the officers we have mentioned. Furthermore, they later added a codicil to the effect that, should these die, other approved men should succeed to their ministry. (44:1-2)

Clement's understanding of the process of succession may be ambiguous, but it is clear that he claims apostolic warrant for a particular governance structure and the official exercise of authority for the sake of unity and the gospel.

The Didache is a set of instructions for the church, probably compiled in Alexandria around A.D. 150 by a Christian writer who edited and combined a catechism and a set of regulations for church order.

The manual on church order, found in chapters 6 through 15, was written at a time when many itinerant prophets and teachers were settling down in a church and were being imitated by pretenders who went from place to place exploiting the respect that the true charismatics had earned. The *Didache* warns the church, at the same time affirming the value of Spirit-inspired speech.

> Welcome every apostle on arriving, as if he were the Lord. But he must not stay beyond one day. In case of necessity, however, the next day too. If he stays three days, he is a false prophet. On departing, an apostle must not accept anything save sufficient food to carry him till his next lodging. If he asks for money, he is a false prophet.
>
> While a prophet is making ecstatic utterances, you must not test or examine him. For "every sin will be forgiven," but this sin "will not be forgiven." However, not everybody making ecstatic utterances is a prophet, but only if he behaves like the Lord. It is by their conduct that the false prophet . . . can be distinguished [from the true prophet]. (11:3-8)

With the increasingly infrequent appearances of the true charismatic itinerants, the *Didache* recognizes provisions for the due selection of officers to succeed them. The transition from a charismatically conceived to an institutionally based church order is evident. When Spirit-inspired proclamation seemed to be disappearing, provision was made for offices in which the gospel and the traditions could be continued under authorized supervision.

Letters of Ignatius. Ignatius, bishop of Antioch, who was on his way to martyrdom in Rome, wrote letters to churches along the way, and to Polycarp, then a young bishop in Smyrna. Chained to a squad of soldiers, Ignatius was taken overland through Asia Minor at some time during the reign of the emperor Trajan (A.D. 98–117).[10]

His letters reveal a man intent not only on preaching the gospel, but upon reflecting Christ's self-giving by following his Lord all the way to the cross. His faith was costing him his life.

The letters reveal, too, a man of deep commitment to the unity of the church and to the authority of the bishop. This hierarchy, according to Ignatius, had divine sanction. In his letter to the Trallians, Ignatius indicates that it is essential that members take no action without the bishop, that they submit to the presbytery (council of elders) and that they show respect to the deacons, who "represent Jesus Christ. . . . The bishop has the role of the Father, and the presbyters are like God's council and an apostolic band. You cannot have a church without these" (3:1). Understanding of church order had moved from a functional definition of offices to an essentially male, divinely sanctioned hierarchy.

In writing to Polycarp, Ignatius describes the episcopal role and responsibilities. The bishop must depend upon God and Jesus to be his own bishops. He is to urge everyone to be saved, give his whole attention to the spiritual and temporal concerns of the congregation, help them, and be patient with them. He is to preserve unity. He is to be in continual prayer, asking for increasing insight, and keeping his spirit alert. Here is no lifeless bureaucratic conception, but an understanding of church order deeply committed to tradition and to life in the Spirit. Thoroughly committed to what he considered a divinely inspired church order, Ignatius calls the followers of Christ to rigorous, disciplined discipleship.

The Apostolic Fathers reflect the progressive institution-alization of the church. Its identity and continuity became increasingly difficult to maintain as the generation of the original apostles disappeared; its unity was threatened by rebellion against established offices. It was clear to the Apostolic Fathers that there was good reason to affirm a divinely grounded church order.

But it is important to remember also that the officers of the church were to be accountable to God for the way they lived and the way they led the church. Bishops were to be deeply spiritual, obedient to Christ, and just and loving in their judgments. Although the hierarchy was firmly established, it is clear that the early church was engaged in fervent and costly witness. Word and Spirit were alive in the hearts, minds, and lives of succeeding generations of the followers of Christ.

Summary

That there was unity and variety of the early church is clear, even in this brief exploration of the first generations of Christianity. Certain crucial aspects of the corporate life are visible:

—the centrality of Jesus Christ;
—the authority of the Word;
—the reality of the Spirit.

Those aspects were expressed in diverse ways, in a variety of theological convictions and patterns of church order; but in those first generations, both Word and Spirit, tradition and gift, were deeply and continually related.

The authority of the earliest apostles came from their relationship with Jesus and their allegiance to him as risen Lord. The power of Paul's witness was derived from his encounter with Christ, who made him an apostle to the Gentiles.

The early church responded to challenges to its integrity not only by defining "approved teaching," but by establishing offices to maintain order. That response was an understandable and apparently appropriate way to deal with internal and external pressures. But the problem was that as the church became involved in maintaining itself, it became increasingly absorbed in its own life—its internal dynamics and structures required increasing attention.

It would be a mistake to assume that such institutionalized Christianity closed off the vitality of the church. The later writings of the New Testament and those of the Apostolic Fathers disclose both the development of the hierarchy and the continuation of an apostolic witness in the world.

Leadership and administration in the early church were shaped by the values and structures of the social systems in which the Christian communities were born and lived—the system of elders in Judaism, the Greek city, the Roman empire. Yet because the gospel was proclaimed and heard in human terms, the Word took root in people's lives and empowered their witness.

The legitimate conclusion of our study is not that just any church order will do. The question is, rather, What kind of leadership and administration allows the Word and the Spirit to direct and empower the community of faith?

CHAPTER 3

The Heritage of
The United Methodist Church

As United Methodists see more clearly who we have been, as we
understand more concretely what are the needs of the world, as
we learn more effectively how to use our heritage and guidelines,
we will become more and more able to fulfill our calling as a
pilgrim people and discern who we may become. (*The Discipline,*
Par. 69)

As we become aware of who we have been, we may
understand more clearly who we are and who we may become.
The purpose of this chapter is to explore the origins of The
United Methodist Church—those periods when the initial
movements were born and organized. As we consider the birth
of those movements and the ways their faith and life were
institutionalized, we may learn more about our own experience. The contemporary character of leadership and administration has its roots in the denomination's origins. In this
chapter we will focus on the Annual Conference, as an early
and important expression of church order and as the setting in
which the church's leadership and administration took initial
and lasting shape. At the close of the chapter we will look at
implications for our life together and the future of leadership
and administration in The United Methodist Church.

We will be dealing with Methodism in England and with the
formation in America of the Methodist Episcopal Church,
the Methodist Protestant Church, the Methodist Episcopal
Church, South, the United Brethren in Christ, and the
Evangelical Association. Although it would be instructive to
follow through the histories of each, we will limit our focus to

those crucial times when renewal movements were generated and given their first institutional expression.

Methodism in England

The Wesleyan movement in England may be described as a renewal movement in the Church of England. John Wesley was born and raised in that established church; his faith and life were formed by his experience as a member of a clergyman's family. It was because he cared so deeply about that church's reformation that he joined religious societies committed to deeper faith and more faithful living.

When he was asked where Methodism began, Wesley cited three major turning points: (1) November 27, 1729, when John and three others met at Oxford University; (b) the second, larger experience in April 1736, in Savannah, Georgia, when twenty or thirty persons gathered at his house and talked about their relationship with God; (c) May 1, 1738, when forty or fifty persons agreed to meet together every Wednesday evening to have free conversation, beginning and ending with song and prayer.

Throughout his life Wesley considered himself a faithful "son of the church," an "extraordinarius," called to revive the Church of England in such a way that clergy and laity would come to their senses. Wesley did not deny, but rather affirmed the "ordinary" means of grace in the sacraments of baptism and the Lord's Supper. He did, however, understand himself as having received a special calling to preach the gospel and to organize people into disciplined societies, composed of those who sought to "flee the wrath to come"—God's judgment on their lives. He believed he was taking on an unused function of the priesthood and hoped to cause such envy or jealousy in the hearts of the established clergy that they would take up their rightful responsibilities and that, as a result, Wesley and his assistants no longer would be needed.

Wesley saw himself as a spiritual guide, or tutor, of those

who came to him for assistance. People who wanted to be "in connection" were welcome to join with him, but when his authority was challenged, he would say that such persons were free to go (and he would be free of them also). Wesley believed that his power to lead was derived from those who granted it to him as their spiritual guide, and in conference, they were encouraged to express their opinions, but the final decisions concerning the Methodist movement lay with him.[1]

Wesley thought of his movement as a means of renewal within the Church of England, and he expected his followers to attend its services and to receive the Lord's Supper regularly from its ordained clergy. But he was convinced also that disciplined societies were useful to the development of Christian life, and in the latter part of 1739, he began weekly meetings—first with a few, then with larger numbers attending.

The societies sprang up in different locations, but under Wesley's leadership, the movement was not a collection of isolated groups. The unifying "connection" was evidenced in Annual Conferences, where Wesley and his fellow clergy met with lay assistants to consider the substance of the faith, the means of its expression, and the requirements of holy living. He recalled that the original Annual Conference took place when he and Charles, together with a small number of lay assistants, met for several days to "consider how we should proceed to save our own souls and those that heard us." In subsequent years, Wesley invited all, but later, only a select number.

> This I did for many years, and all that time the term "Conference" meant not so much the conversation we had together as the persons that conferred—namely, those whom I invited to confer with me from time to time. So that all this depended on me alone, not only what persons should constitute the conference, but whether there should be any Conference at all. This lay wholly in my own breast; neither the preachers nor the people having any part in the matter.[2]

The "Minutes of the First Annual Conference," which met at the Foundry in London, in June of 1744, record that on Sunday, June 24, the clergy and lay preachers shared Communion, and on Monday, Charles Wesley preached before the opening session.

> After some time spent in prayer, the design of our meeting was proposed, namely, to consider:
> 1. What to teach;
> 2. How to teach, and
> 3. What to do, i.e. how to regulate doctrine, discipline and practice.[3]

The content of the discussion was summarized in question-and-answer form in the "Minutes" and dealt with doctrine, relationship to the Church of England, and ordering of the movement, including the work of the lay assistants. The substance of the conference, according to Albert Outler, was the consideration of *message* (what to teach), *method* (how to teach), and *ethos* (how to live).

Wesley, influenced by his father and other "convocation men," was convinced that genuine church leadership comes not from humans alone, but must originate in the Holy Spirit. Wesley admired the Moravian *conferenz* and believed it would be especially useful for the Church of England, which he considered far too large and its bishops far too busy. The Moravian fellowship was voluntary, but having joined, the individual was part of the whole, and individual preferences were subordinated to the consensus of the body. The *conferenz* was highly structured and included many offices, with well-defined roles and responsibilities. Thus Wesley affirmed both divine leadership and human responsibility in his leadership of the Annual Conference.

Wesley believed that church government should originate from the Word proclaimed and heard and that the necessities of nurture should be supplied by helpers/deacons working under the supervision of elders, the whole directed by Wesley, their common "father in God." Wesley was convinced that the generation of the United Societies paralleled the experience of the apostolic church, but that the form of church governance was a matter of "good order," established by reason, rather than a matter essentially of Christian faith.

Annual Conferences continued without interruption in England during and after Wesley's lifetime. The "Minutes" contain a compelling record of a movement committed to the renewal of the Church of England, but forced to proclaim the gospel and develop new forms of corporate life outside the established church. The character of the movement's leadership and administration grew out of that experience.

Methodism Comes to America

The Methodist movement first spread to the American colonies through immigrants from England and Ireland, under the leadership of lay people such as Barbara Heck, Philip Embury, and Thomas Webb, who started societies without Wesley's official permission.

In 1769, in response to a request from American Methodists, Wesley asked the British Annual Conference for volunteers from among the traveling preachers to serve in "the wilderness of America." Richard Boardman and Joseph Pilmoor agreed to go and began their ministries in New York and Philadelphia. But it was Francis Asbury who was to take the major responsibility for establishing the Methodist movement in America.

In American Methodism, a "congregation" sometimes consisted of hundreds, but a "society" was organized only after careful preparation and was composed of fewer than thirty members.[4] Certified members of the societies received membership tickets admitting them to meetings and to "love-feasts," which were occasions for prayer, singing, and testimony, during a fellowship meal of bread and water.

Quarterly meetings were held in many areas and consisted of all the local preachers and lay leaders, as well as other members of a society or circuit. The sessions included prayer;

singing; testimony; agendas that dealt with collections, stationing and support of preachers, and standards for admission to the societies; and administration of the Sacraments by ordained clergy of the Church of England.

The first conference of American Methodists was held July 14 through 16, 1773, at St. George's Church in Philadelphia. Thomas Rankin, then Wesley's general assistant in America, presided over the gathering, which included Asbury among the preachers. The "Minutes" reaffirm Wesley's authority and affirm "the doctrine and discipline of the Methodists as contained in the minutes of the Annual Conferences in Britain to be the sole rule of our conduct, who labor in connection with Mr. Wesley in America."[5]

Although the Annual Conference shared with its British counterpart its convictions concerning doctrinal matters and organizational forms, in America the conference itself grew to be sovereign, refusing to send reports of its actions to Wesley for his approval. The Annual Conference decided by majority vote, matters that, in Britain, were determined by Wesley alone. This assertion of conference authority was a major step in the adaptation of Methodism to the democratic spirit of American life and thought. Even Asbury, who later was to act in a manner some found autocratic, complained that Thomas Rankin was not giving him due consideration in the matter of his appointment.

With the close of the Revolutionary War and the ending of ties with the British government and the Church of England, American Methodist leaders were no longer in a position to require their members to take Communion from Anglican priests. Wesley, recognizing the dilemma, took the extraordinary step of appointing superintendents and elders for America, that they might establish continuity of leadership and ordain Methodist preachers to administer the Sacraments. He concluded that, with the precedent set by the early church in Alexandria, not only bishops but elders, also, were properly authorized to ordain clergy. Having struggled for many years with the issues and consequences of such actions,

Wesley, confronted by what he considered necessity, appointed Americans Thomas Coke and Francis Asbury as superintendents and ordained British Richard Whatcoat and Thomas Vasey to go to America to serve as elders. In his letter "to Our Brethren in America" Wesley confirmed what he had done and concluded, "They are now at full liberty to follow the scriptures and the primitive church. And we judge it best that they should stand in that liberty wherein God has made them so strangely free."[6]

Shortly after they landed, Whatcoat and Vasey met Asbury to inform him of his appointment, but Asbury refused to accept the position unless the preachers unanimously chose him to serve in that capacity. It was determined that a meeting should be held, and on December 17, 1784, Asbury, Whatcoat, and Coke met to set the agenda of what later would be called the Christmas Conference.

The traveling preachers were invited, and those who could come met on December 24, at Lovely Lane Chapel in Baltimore. Thomas Coke presided and read Wesley's letter. "The Methodist Episcopal Church" was selected as the official name, and the body determined that there should be three orders of ministry (deacons, elders, and superintendents), that ordination should be by the imposition of hands by the superintendents and elders, and that the ritual Wesley had prepared should be accepted for the American Methodists.

Asbury was ordained deacon, elder, and superintendent, respectively, on December 26, 27, and 28, and an additional fourteen deacons and twelve elders were ordained as well. The superintendents were given the responsibility of presiding at sessions of the Annual Conference and of fixing the appointments of preachers during the intervals between sessions. Superintendents were to be amenable to the conference, which had the authority to expel them for improper conduct, and were, moreover, to be itinerants, together with the other traveling preachers. If superintendents ceased to travel, they no longer could exercise any ministerial function.

The Discipline adopted by the Christmas Conference provided for elders to administer the Sacraments and perform other rituals; deacons were to baptize and assist in the administration of the Lord's Supper; and helpers were to preach, meet with the society and "bands" (smaller, more disciplined groups), visit the sick, and meet regularly with the leaders. The "assistant" was a preacher appointed by the superintendent to assist him and the other preachers in a circuit.

Asbury had already envisioned the development of new churches in the new nation. He had seen that nation come to birth, and understood that if it survived there would be churches, and those churches would have to be utterly independent of the state and therefore self-sufficient. In order to be self-sufficient they would have to maximize their mission. In order to maximize its mission, the Methodist Episcopal Church would have to maximize its personnel, and the Annual Conference was conceived of as an annual re-determination of how to get the mission done with the available personnel with optimal effectiveness. The circuit riders already had their message, and there was next to no theological dissent about this message. Thus the method and ethos of their mission were their crucial questions.[7]

To a great extent, Asbury was responsible for the formation of an ordered and disciplined Methodist itineracy in America—apostolic in spirit, episcopal in polity. Frontier Methodists, without official authority, often had formed societies before the itinerant ministers came. With the energy and discipline the traveling preachers brought, new congregations and societies emerged, almost in geometric proportion, within a connectional system.[8]

The 1813 *Minutes* of the New England Conference reveal a larger membership, a more complex agenda, and a decision-making process that utilized committees for evaluations and recommendations concerning difficult matters. The conference was involved not only with "ministerial matters," but with policy issues—these had to do with congregations that were building elaborate structures and selling reserved seats

to the wealthy members of the church. Buildings, the
conference decided, should be plain, decent, and inexpen-
sive. Pews were not to be sold. Congregations that failed to
heed those injunctions were to expect to have their
connection with the denomination severed.

By the early part of the nineteenth century, the Methodist
movement in America had become the Methodist Episcopal
Church, with provisions for its life and ministry spelled out in
a *Discipline* adopted by the General Conference. Led by
bishops, the Annual Conferences, too, had taken on a more
formal character and provided supervision for preachers and
congregations in an increasingly complex connectional
system.

The Methodist Protestant Church

John Wesley, during his lifetime, was the acknowledged
head of the United Societies in England. He saw no need to
provide for the "democratic rights" of the preachers and no
point to permitting the laity to choose their preachers.
American Methodists did resist Wesley's autocratic perspective, but Asbury, too, was manifestly uninterested in
representative church government. For him, the Revolutionary War was simply an interruption, democratic rights
not being suitable for "spiritual" church government.

Since its introduction into America, there have been
preachers who resisted the established appointive process.
James O'Kelly, in the Annual Conference of 1784, proposed
that preachers be permitted to appeal to the conference if
they were dissatisfied with their appointments. O'Kelly's
motion was defeated, but the democratic spirit continued, in
spite of such warnings as the 1792 conference action, which
determined that any member convicted of sowing dissension
should be expelled from the Society. But the "reformers"
continued to advocate changes in the appointive system and
also advocated conference membership, not only for local
pastors, but for lay people as well.

George Brown, an early leader in the protest movement, recounted a memorable evening when a presiding elder of the Methodist Episcopal Church took tea with a physician, a Dr. Stanton, whose wife was a member of the church. The elder asked the doctor why he had not joined. The doctor replied that he approved of Methodist doctrine and meetings, but not of its government, which lay solely in the hands of the clergy. The elder illustrated what he considered to be the marvelous polity of the denomination, comparing it to the machinery of a mill:

> There is one great all-moving wheel which describes a large circle (at the same time making a circular motion with his hands), and that is the episcopal wheel. Within this large wheel are other wheels moving in due subordination to it, and they are the presiding elder wheels. With in each of these there are many other wheels, all in harmonious operation, and they are the circuit and stationed preacher wheels. Within each of these again are a diversity of wheels, all operating to admiration, and they are the local preacher, exhorter and class-leader wheels. So, like Ezekiel's vision, wheel within wheel, the entire system moves on with the most perfect regularity and harmony. O, it is the best government in the world.
>
> For a moment I thought the doctor worsted, and my feelings stood redeemed. But he replied, "Aye, and all these wheels to grind the people. . . . Your government is more tyrannical than that of Britain, which our fathers threw off, at the expense of much blood and treasure. . . . I can never consent to sustain any system so contrary to the rights of mankind, or the liberties of my country."[9]

On November 12, 1828, a General Convention of Methodist Reformers was held in Baltimore, with ninety-five delegates, most of whom were from Maryland, with several from other states as well. The doctrine, general rules, ritual, and moral discipline of the Methodist Episcopal Church were accepted, but autonomy was granted to local churches in matters of admission to membership and the holding of property. Provision was made for equal numbers of lay and ministerial representatives at sessions of the Annual Conference.

The conference determined to elect annually a president, rather than a bishop, to preside and to travel throughout the area, so as to be present at quarterly conferences during the year. The president was empowered to ordain elders and, with the consent of the pastors involved, to make changes in their assignments between conference sessions.

The Methodist Episcopal Church, South

The regional divison of Methodists which produced the Methodist Episcopal Church, South, was precipitated by a controversy over slavery, but raised a number of other issues as well, including the relationship of church and state and the authority of the episcopacy.

The General Conference of the Methodist Episcopal Church in 1844 was a watershed in the denomination's history. At the time, there were five bishops—among them, James Andrew, who had acquired two young slaves from his first wife's estate. He lived in Georgia, where manumission (the freeing of slaves) was officially prohibited. *The Discipline,* reflecting Wesley's assessment of slavery as "an execrable villany," forbade slave ownership by Methodists, but qualified its opposition by allowing it to continue in states were manumission was prohibited by law. Amid much anxiety and hostility, the delegates from the southern Annual Conferences refused to accept the decision, and a plan of separation was drawn up. On May 1, 1845, delegates from twelve Annual Conferences and an Indian mission met in Louisville with bishops Soule and Andrew, to establish boundaries and lay the groundwork for a conference the following year in Virginia. Thus the Methodist Episcopal Church, South, was established at a General Conference in May of 1846.

The division in the denomination also reflected different understandings of the episcopacy. At the 1844 General Conference, the Conference Party insisted on the supremacy of the General Conference—that its bishops were accountable for their behavior and subject to its instruction. The

Constitution Party, supported primarily by southerners but including some northerners, maintained that the episcopacy was a coequal branch—subject to trial or misconduct, but not subject to the General Conference.

Albert Outler, reflecting on southern bishops and the Annual Conferences, states:

> In the southern church there was always a history of strong bishops, and of strong policies made by strong bishops, implemented by General Conference, which were then reflected, assimilated, translated, transvaluated in Annual Conference. The Annual Conference in the Southern tradition is still the gathering of representative Christians concerned with how the leadership envisages the message, how the leadership manages the method of itineracy and connectionalism, and how the Annual Conference understands its ethos, always as it supports the primary aims of mission, in and to the world.[10]

As northern Methodism developed agencies for administration of the denomination's program, the southern church affirmed the authority of its bishops in determining the direction of the church's ministry and mission.

United Brethren in Christ

The roots of the United Brethren in Christ may be traced to Philip William Otterbein, a clergyman in the Reformed Church who had come to America as a missionary among the German immigrants. Otterbein served as pastor of a number of Reformed congregations in Pennsylvania and Maryland, and in 1774, received a call to a separatist church in Baltimore, which had withdrawn from the Reformed Church in a dispute over "the lifeless and unedifying preaching and offensive life" of a former pastor.

The second major figure in the early history of the United Brethren was Martin Boehm. Boehm went preaching among the German immigrants in Maryland, Pennsylvania, and Virginia, joining with other Mennonite, Moravian, and

Dunkard pastors in that evangelical movement called the Second Great Awakening. Boehm's continued association with ministers of congregations other than "peace" churches made him suspect among the Mennonites, and in 1780 he was expelled from their company. But he continued to preach while maintaining his farm, and eventually he built a chapel there for the use of both ordained and unordained preachers of many denominations in proclaiming an evangelical gospel.

"Great Meetings" were assemblies called by the Dunkards, or German baptists, in the farming areas around Lancaster during the 1760s, for protracted periods of preaching and fellowship. On Pentecost, 1767, when Boehm was invited to preach, Otterbein was present. Following the service, greatly moved, he went forward and grasped Boehm, declaring *"Wir sind Brudern"* (We are brethren), and thus began a relationship that was to last the remainder of their lives.[11]

When Otterbein became pastor of the Evangelical Reformed Church in Baltimore, he was asked to provide leadership not only for that congregation but for other evangelical churches in Pennsylvania, Maryland, and Virginia. His contact with likeminded preachers led eventually to conferences.

The first formal Annual Conference of the United Brethren in Christ was held on September 25, 1800, in Frederick, Maryland. The *Minutes* record the presence of Otterbein, Boehm, and twelve other preachers including William Newcomer, whose journal recorded the following action:

> Resolved that yearly a day shall be appointed when the unsectarian *(unparteiische)* preachers shall assemble and counsel how they may conduct their office more and more according to the will of God, and according to the mind of God, that the church of God may be built up, so that God in Christ may be honored.[12]

Later records indicate that Otterbein and Boehm were elected, or at least thought of by the preachers at that conference, as bishops or superintendents.

United Brethren polity was adapted from the Methodist Episcopal *Discipline*. The first United Brethren *Discipline* provided for quadrennial General Conferences, which elected bishops for four-year terms. The Annual Conference was responsible for "ministerial matters" and for the stationing of pastors by the bishop, with the assistance of presiding elders who were elected for two-year terms. Both itinerant and local pastors were conference members. Through the careful assistance of Newcomer and others, the informal fellowship became an established denomination and its Annual Conference the center of an enduring ministry.

The Evangelical Association

Jacob Albright was born in 1759 to a German Lutheran immigrant couple who had settled west of Philadelphia. In 1791, in a prayer meeting, he experienced God's saving love. He then joined a Methodist class meeting and was granted an exhorter's license. Although not formally educated, he became a student of the Scriptures—an orderly and able man whose religious convictions were expressed through both his preaching and his way of life.

The Second Great Awakening was largely rural and led primarily by lay preachers. It was a democratic movement, in the spirit of Jeffersonian equality, and it was within this context that Albright's People came into being.[13]

Albright preached and formed class meetings. Among those who responded were John Walter and George Miller, who became itinerant preachers, sharing in Albright's work among German immigrants. In 1803 Albright and his two assistants met with fourteen other lay people in Berks County, Pennsylvania. They declared themselves a "society," adopted the Scriptures as their guide, and ordained Albright as elder through the laying on of hands.

Albright continued to provide leadership for the movement, meeting informally with the preachers and appointing them to circuits. In 1806 Albright, Miller, and Walter saw the need for "being bound together" and made a covenant, renewed later that year through a written contract.[14] By 1807 the society had 220 members, and the first "regular" Annual Conference was held in the home of Samuel Becker in Lebanon County, Pennsylvania. Five itinerant and three local preachers were present, together with 23 class leaders and exhorters. They organized themselves as The Newly Constituted Methodist Conference and authorized the preparation of a *Discipline* similar to that of the Methodists. The conference elected Albright as bishop, George Miller as elder, and John Dreisbach and Jacob Frey as preachers on trial.

Following Albright's death, George Miller provided direction for the movement and by 1809 had prepared the "Rules of Faith and Order," the *Discipline,* and a catechism, for action by the Annual Conference. They adopted The So-Called Albright's People as their name, reflecting the uncertainty about their status as a denomination. Their *Discipline* did, however, make them identifiable, so that Miller could say, "Many others were induced to unite with us and work out their soul's salvation."[15]

Conference leadership was in the form of an elected president and secretary. Only itinerate preachers were allowed to vote, although local preachers and class leaders were present as well. The conference session included rigorous examination of the character of all the preachers.

As the number of preachers and churches increased, more complex issues presented themselves, and the Annual Conference of 1816 appointed twelve men to meet later to deal with such matters, in what eventually became a General Conference. They chose the name Evangelical Association, utilizing the German *gemeinschaft,* rather than "church," to reflect the covenantal nature of the relationship.

Dreisbach met Asbury, who was impressed with the young man and invited him to join the Methodist Annual Conference. Dreisbach countered with a proposal that the followers of Albright join with the Methodists in a separate conference for German-speaking people, but Asbury indicated that such a plan would not be "expedient." Though the merger did not take place, Asbury and Dreisbach remained friends.

The Evangelical Association developed after 1839 under bishops elected quadrennially by the General Conference for four-year, renewable terms. The salaries of the itinerant preachers initially were equalized, but by the middle of the century, varying salaries were paid to the pastors directly by local churches, rather than by the previous system of a central treasury.

Sessions of the Annual Conferences included the appointment of preachers, who originally were stationed by a committee of from three to five clergy appointed annually by the conference. Subsequently, the Annual Conference elected presiding elders who were to serve four-year terms, have "superintendence" over the temporal and spiritual concerns of the society, attend quarterly meetings of the church, plan and conduct tent meetings, and provide information for the bishop, who became responsible for making the appointments.

Summary

The origins of The United Methodist Church may be found in renewal movements that developed into established denominations. From this brief survey, we find a number of issues that are crucial to the understanding of our current leadership and administration.

1. At the heart of the renewal movements were some extraordinarily sensitive men and women who heard the gospel speaking to them, who found themselves changed by the Spirit, and who were empowered to use their gifts to share the good news.

2. The charismatic founders of the movements formed small groups—disciplined covenant communities. Such fellowships contributed to the deepening of faith and served as bases for strategic engagement in witness.

3. At the birth of a movement, the goals were understood in clear and compelling ways. Grounded in the Scriptures, the message was sounded in understandable and life-changing terms and generated lives of "vital piety."

4. The "connection"—that interdependent network of relationships among people and groups—provided a sustained and accountable structure for a movement's growth.

5. There was ambivalence toward leadership, which affirmed the founders, but which eventually limited their power through conferences where American democratic sensitivities were expressed.

6. The movements were missionary orders, composed of people who had moved out of established churches to proclaim the gospel in the world.

7. The movements began with a clear sense of divine initiative—with people who believed that the providence of God was at work through them, sustaining them in difficulty and making their witness effective.

8. The Annual Conference served as a catalyst for the movements and as a focus for the establishment of the denominations. In America, it was not a forum for theological debate, but a covenant community of preachers who were committed to the gospel and to one another.

9. Lay leadership, through lay preachers and class leaders, was present from the very beginning of the movements, although the laity was not represented in sessions of the Annual Conference.

10. Though there were regional and denominational differences in the understanding of the episcopacy, bishops emerged as potent leaders and administrators, symbolizing the faith and commitment of the church.

The faith and the order of the early movements of United Methodism reflected the founders' convictions of the centrality of Christ, the authority of the Word, and the power of the Spirit. Leadership and administration were developed to engage the communities of faith in vigorous and sustained apostolic witness. Word and Spirit—tradition and spiritual gifts—were affirmed by charismatic leadership set free and sustained by the gospel.

The "connection" provided the fabric for the emerging denominations and was designed to maintain the vitality of both Word and Spirit. As in the early church, the early United Methodist movements were shaped by their own time and culture, their inherited faith, and the order of the established religious communities from which they emerged. As in the early church, the movements became institutions; they established patterns of authority and offices for leadership and administration. The dangers of preoccupation with institutional maintenance were present from the beginning, and those who originated the movements generally were aware of such problems. In fact, the designs for leadership and administration were shaped by a commitment to apostolic Christianity and an aversion to the self-serving forms of institutional church life that diminish the vitality of the Christian community.

CHAPTER 4

The Annual Conference—
Its Leadership and Administration:
The Official Position

In the search for a better understanding of leadership and administration, we have explored developments of church order in the early church and in the movements that became the denominations which constitute The United Methodist Church. Our purpose is not simply to recite intriguing stories, but to find within the events and the stories those enduring realities that shape our current experience and provide direction for the future.

Leadership and administration are exercised in particular situations, and we are convinced that a deeper understanding of the governance of the church may be achieved not only by a clearer perception of our heritage, but by a comprehensive look at the currently experienced realities of church order.

The Annual Conference continues to be a strategic arena for corporate life in the "connection," and in order to view the present leadership and administration in that context, we move to an examination of the official structures, policies, and procedures that govern the conference. *The Discipline* is the "canon law" of the denomination, reflecting the accumulated commitments and compromises in the history of The United Methodist Church; in matters of church order, United Methodists generally have accepted *The Discipline*. Therefore we will study the Disciplinary provisions for the Annual Conference, since we believe that a firmer grasp of the official position may help us understand what is happening and why people feel the way they do. In addition, any suggestions concerning principles and models for the future must consider the given realities, and one of those is *The Discipline.*

Constitutional Provisions

The constitution of The United Methodist Church defines the functions of the Annual Conference. The designation of the Annual Conference as "the basic body" (Par. 37) of The United Methodist Church is made in light of (a) the control that Annual Conference members collectively exercise in relation to constitutional amendments; (b) the power available to Annual Conference delegates to the General Conference, which serves as the basic legislative body of the denomination, and to the Jurisdictional (or Central [overseas]) Conferences, which elect and assign bishops; (c) the authority of its ministerial members to determine matters of ministerial relations; and (d) the role of the Annual Conference as a repository for all other powers not reserved to the General Conference in the constitution.

The "Preamble to the Constitution" states some basic theological convictions concerning the nature of mission of the Church.

> The Church is a community of all true believers under the Lordship of Christ. It is the redeemed and redeeming fellowship in which the Word of God is preached by persons divinely called, and the Sacraments are duly administered according to Christ's own appointment. Under the discipline of the Holy Spirit the Church seeks to provide for the maintenance of worship, the edification of believers, and the redemption of the world. (p. 19)

Subsequent paragraphs affirm the denomination's self-understanding as part of the Church Universal—the United Methodist commitment to unity with all Christians—as well as its racial, social, and economic inclusiveness. The preamble provides a theological perspective for understanding the church and its life and order.

Conference Membership

Part 4 of *The Discipline,* dealing with the organization and administration of the denomination, begins with a chapter on "The Ministry of All Christians." The heart of the Christian ministry is understood in terms of servanthood expressed in "a common life of gratitude and devotion, witness and service, celebration, and discipleship" (Par. 101). Within the community of the New Covenant, all Christians are called to minister. That "general ministry" is a gift of God's grace, acknowledged in baptism, ratified in confirmation, and fulfilled in unstinting service. "The people of God are the Church made visible in the world. It is they who must convince the world of the reality of the gospel or leave it unconvinced" (Par. 106). Within that general ministry, there are laypersons, diaconal ministers (consecrated to ministries of love, justice, and service), and ordained ministers (ordained to the ministry of Word, Sacrament, and order).

The lay people of the Annual Conference are "members," not "delegates" required to represent the majority views of their congregations or the other bodies from which they were selected. Only lay members may vote on lay delegates to the General and Jurisdictional (or Central) conferences. Lay members are eligible to vote on all matters, with the exception of ministerial relations. *The Discipline* affirms the role of the laity by stipulating that, with the exception of the Board of Ordained Ministry, all conference councils, boards, and agencies shall be composed of one-third laywomen, one-third laymen, and one-third clergy.

Ordained ministers are not members of a local church, but of an Annual Conference.

Members in full connection with an Annual Conference by virtue of their election and ordination are bound in special covenant with all the ordained ministers of the Annual Conference. In the keeping of this covenant they perform the ministerial duties and maintain the ministerial standards established by those in the covenant. They offer themselves without reserve to be appointed and to serve, after consultation, as the appointive authority may determine. They live with their fellow ordained ministers in mutual trust and concern and seek with them the sanctification of the fellowship. Only those shall be elected to full membership who are of unquestionable moral character and genuine piety, sound in the fundamental doctrines of Christianity and faithful in the discharge of their duties. (Par. 422)

Thus the Annual Conference provides a continuing denominational context and covenant for ministerial members— willing to serve under episcopal appointment, bound to mutual support and accountability. Associate members (ministerial) are those who have not met the requirements for full membership but who may be ordained deacon and vote on all matters except those reserved to full members.

Local pastors are included in the minsterial membership of an Annual Conference if they are serving under full-time appointment to a pastoral charge. These local pastors have the right to vote, except on constitutional amendments, election of delegates to General and Jurisdictional (or Central) conferences, and ministerial matters.

Although diaconal ministers are not conference members in the same sense as the ordained clergy, the Annual Conference does provide an enduring denominational relationship in which they are consecrated by the bishop. The conference Board of Diaconal Ministry recommends them and holds them accountable for the faithful exercise of their specialized ministries of service within the church's life and mission.

Functions and Organization of the Annual Conference

The Discipline specifies under "Business of the Conference" that there shall be an opening period of devotion and a roll call of lay and ministerial members, local pastors, and diaconal ministers. An agenda, prepared by the bishop and others, is to be submitted to the conference for adoption and is to include the hearing and acting upon of "reports from the district superintendents, the officers, the standing and special committees, the boards, commissions, and societies and also the making of such inquiries as the Council of Bishops shall recommend by the provision of a supplemental guide" (Par. 704.4). The most detailed list of responsibilities is found in the "Disciplinary Questions," which sums up the matter of organization and business, ministerial relations, and appointments which the Annual Conference must report to the general church.

The Development of Ministry. The conference Board of Ministry is responsible for recruitment, training, ordination, and conference relations of ministerial members and local pastors. *The Discipline* indicates that the Annual Conference also is responsible for inquiring into the moral and official conduct of its ministers—"whether all ministerial members of the conference are blameless in their life and official administration" (Par. 704.5). Either the district superintendents or the Board of Ministry may report on such matters, in a plenary session of the Annual Conference or in an "executive session" of ministerial members only.

The historic requirements for itinerant ministerial members are reflected in the questions John Wesley posed to the traveling preachers in his time. The bishop, at each session of the conference, repeats those questions to persons seeking admission, having explained their "historic nature . . . spirit and intent."

The ministry of the laity is recognized through the office of the conference lay leader, who is to foster awareness of the laity in the mission of the church and facilitate lay participation in a cooperative ministry with the clergy at all levels of the church. Various conference agencies are responsible for equipping and supporting the laity in their ministry and mission. Conference lay organizations also include an optional United Methodist Men, a Council on Youth Ministry, and a United Methodist Women, related to the Women's Division of the Board of Global Ministries.

Program Development. The Discipline allocates program

responsibilities to a variety of conference agencies, including a Council on Ministries, which is to receive program recommendations from all levels of the church, develop them into a coordinated program, and provide for their implementation and administration. The Council on Ministries integrates the work of conference agencies and maintains the connectional relationships of program units at the local church, district, conference, and national levels.

There is considerable flexibility in Annual Conference structure so that it may meet its Disciplinary responsibilities, maintain contact with United Methodist educational, health, and welfare agencies, and fulfill its strategic role in the connectional system.

Financial Management. The Annual Conference is a vital link in the generation, budgeting, and allocation of the financial resources of The United Methodist Church. The major responsibility belongs to the conference Council on Finance and Administration and to the conference treasurer, who is the representative of the council. In addition, a business manager or administrator may be employed to assist in the management of conference affairs.

The council prepares a budget for consideration by the Annual Conference, including the amounts required as a result of action by the General and Jurisdictional conferences. The council studies the needs and causes of the conference, considers program budgets recommended by the Council on Ministries, and includes amounts specified by the Board of Pensions. Local churches are responsible for financial support of the budget through payment of amounts apportioned to them. A majority of the council's membership are laypersons.

Church Property Management. The Discipline provides that all church property shall be held in trust for The United Methodist Church and subject to its *Discipline.* The Annual Conference board of trustees is empowered to receive and hold trust funds and property given to the conference. It is responsible for acquiring and maintaining an episcopal residence, as well as other conference properties.

In the event that an Annual Conference determines that a local church is to be discontinued, the trustees are to sell or dispose of that property, with the consent of the bishop, a majority of the superintendents, and the district Board of Church Location and Building.

Annual Conference Leadership and Administration

The glossary in *The Discipline* defines the Annual Conference as "the basic administrative body in The United Methodist Church, bearing responsibility for the work of the Church in a specific territory as established by the Jurisdictional or Central Conference" (p. 640). This definition reflects the Disciplinary understanding of the authority of the Annual Conference as a corporate body. Administration is not simply a function of the bishop or of individuals elected or appointed to serve in offices. The conference itself, as a conciliar unit comprised of clergy and lay people, has administrative authority.

Conference officers include the bishop, one of whose "presidential" responsibilities is to preside at sessions of the conference. The Annual Conference elects a secretary, statistician and treasurer, and a chancellor, if it chooses, to provide legal assistance. Conference boards, agencies, and organizations also elect officers to provide leadership and administrative functions, facilitating cooperation with all levels of the connectional system.

The conference director of the Council on Ministries is responsible for the complex task of planning, coordinating, and implementing conference program. He or she serves in a consultative relationship with the cabinet (bishop and district superintendents) but does not participate in making ministerial appointments. A conference may employ additional staff to facilitate its work.

The Meaning of the Superintendency. In The United

Methodist Church, "superintendency" refers to the supervision of the temporal and spiritual welfare of the denomination by its bishops and district superintendents (Par. 501).

Bishops and superintendents are expected to fulfill the major leadership and administrative roles in the temporal and spiritual life of the church. *The Discipline* states that the offices of bishop and superintendent are particular ministries for which persons are elected or selected from among ordained elders. As ministers of Christ, they share in a royal priesthood which has apostolic roots (I Peter 2:9; John 21:15-17; Acts 20:28; I Peter 5:2-3; I Tim. 3:1-7), and as elders, they are required to share in ministries of Word and Sacrament, as well as order.

The Discipline specifies the particular abilities, skills, and disciplines required of the superintendency. These include the ability to read consensus and integrate it into a living tradition and to be open to the prophetic Word. Persons in those offices are required to cultivate forms of accountability through a support group and to possess skill in team building and negotiation. They should practice spiritual discipline and be capable of theological reflection. They must be able to analyze, plan, and organize resources and evaluate program and personnel. They are to take time for reflection, study, friendships, and self-renewal. "The style of leadership should rise out of nurtured and cultivated spiritual disciplines and patterns of holiness, for the Spirit is given to the community and its members to the extent that they participate" (Par. 502.1).

Bishops. Bishops are considered "general superintendents" of The United Methodist Church, providing leadership for the whole denomination through their participation in the connectional system at all levels and around the world. The Council of Bishops at the general church level, and the College of Bishops in each jurisdiction, provide corporate contexts for episcopal responsibility. The bishop's "presidential" duties include presiding not only at sessions of the Annual Conference, but at the Jurisdictional (or Central) and

General conferences as well. It is the bishops who consecrate those elected to the episcopacy.

The bishop's "residential" duties in an Annual Conference encompass the ordination of deacons and elders, consecration of diaconal ministers, and the commissioning of deaconesses and home missionaries; the major "residential" function is the appointment of ordained ministers and local pastors. Bishops also are responsible for dividing and uniting circuits, stations, or missions; fixing the Charge Conference membership of ministers serving beyond the local church; reading the appointments of deaconesses, diaconal ministers, and home missionaries; transferring ministerial members from one conference to another; forming districts, after their number has been determined by the Annual Conference; appointing district superintendents; facilitating ecumenical and interfaith relationships; and engaging the Annual Conference in matters of social concern.

Bishops do not constitute a "third order" in the denomination, but serve as elders elected to that office by the Jurisdictional (or Central) Conferences. The Annual Conference may nominate persons for consideration, but election to the episcopacy is not limited to those persons. Bishops are elected for life, but generally serve no more than eight consecutive years in the same area (composed of one or more Annual Conferences). The Jurisdictional Committee on the Episcopacy, comprised of equal numbers of ministerial and lay representatives of the Annual Conferences, submits to the Jurisdictional (or Central) Conference its recommendations for the assignment of bishops to particular areas. *The Discipline* provides an Annual Conference Committee on the Episcopacy to assist and support the bishop in fulfilling episcopal responsibilities within the conference.

District Superintendents. The district superintendency is an extension of the episcopacy. The bishop appoints elders to serve as superintendents, *The Discipline* specifying that due consideration be given in respect to race, sex, and national origin. Superintendents are to serve in that office for no more than six in nine consecutive years, and not more than twice.

District superintendents are to oversee the total ministry of the pastors and churches in their districts; give pastoral support and supervision to the clergy and encourage their spiritual and professional growth; and through programs, to assist local churches in their ministry and mission. Superintendents are to be of service to the bishop in the administration of the conference, in consultation with other conference officers and agencies; their major responsibility is to be of help to the bishop in making appointments.

> Pastors and clergy in extension ministries shall be appointed by a bishop, who is empowered to make and fix all appointments in the episcopal area within which the Annual Conference is a part. Appointments are to be made with consideration of gifts, graces of those appointed, to the needs, characteristics, and opportunities of congregations and institutions, and to program and missional strategy of conferences and without regard to race, ethnic origin, sex, or color, consistent with the commitment to an open itinerary. Through appointment-making, the connectional nature of the United Methodist system is made visible. (Par. 527.1)

Appointment-making is to be accomplished with appropriate consultation with the parties involved, but *The Discipline* clearly indicates that ultimately, it is the responsibility of the bishop to make the appointment, based on the information and advice received. All existing appointments are to be reported at every session of the Annual Conference, but the bishop, with the assistance of the superintendents, may make changes at any time.

Summary

In terms of *The Discipline,* the Annual Conference may be understood as a unit in the connectional system of The United Methodist Church, which is part of the Church Universal. It provides a regional center for program development and for financial and property management; a context for the appointment of ministers and for the supervision of both churches and clergy. It serves as a covenant community for ordained ministerial members and as a denominational context for diaconal ministers. The Annual Conference is basic in the system of conferences which links the denomination together.

The Discipline provides grounds for the conclusion that leadership and administration in the Annual Conference are:

1. highly connectional (strategically related to the whole denomination);
2. clergy-oriented (the bishop, superintendents, and ordained clergy fulfill almost all major roles);
3. oriented more toward administering (implementing and supervising) than toward leading (generating faith and envisioning the future).

Provisions in *The Discipline* do not reflect significant attention toward either Word or Spirit, though there are references to preaching and spiritual life. The structure and roles of the Annual Conference are described in functional terms, instrumental to the mission and ministry of the church. Clearly there is need for such functions, but unless they are deeply related to Word and Spirit, the apostolic power of the denomination is diminished, and the offices of the church are secularized.

Originally, the Annual Conference functioned as a gathering, to enable a missionary order to be clear about what to teach, how to teach, and how to live. Understandable changes have come as movements were institutionalized and became denominations, but *The Discipline* provides substance for concluding that the leadership and administration of the Annual Conference is directed systematically more toward maintenance than toward mission. In further chapters, we will consider what we found as we observed sessions of Annual Conferences and heard from lay people, bishops, superintendents, pastors, and those in special appointments.

CHAPTER 5

Perceptions and Hypotheses About the Present

"Perception" tends to have two complementary meanings: (a) awareness of the elements of environment through physical sensation; and (b) quick, acute, intuitive, cognition and appreciation. Carl Jung postulated also that fundamentally, there are two different ways to perceive—to get in touch with the reality that surrounds us. He described those two ways as *sensing* and *intuition*. By "sensing," he referred to the collecting of data through the five physical senses: *sight, sound, touch, smell, taste.* "Intuition" is the capacity to take in a *whole* situation, to have immediate hunches, to speculate about future possibilities.[1]

Obviously, in our common humanity, we share in both these methods of perception. All of us (to a greater or lesser extent) have the ability to see, hear, touch, smell, and taste—plus the sense of intuition. We prefer to use and trust either one or the other—but both we have.

How This Study Gathered Its Perceptions

In this study, we have utilized both methods to try to get in touch with the way The United Methodist Church sees itself—its leaders and administrators. Based on sensing, we have

—watched the church in action—in Annual Conference meetings, in conference headquarters, in seminaries, in local churches. We have read its history, its *Discipline,* and the data of other studies.

—heard the church talk to itself and to others, in sermons, addresses, resolutions, arguments, and small talk.

—stood in the places where the church walks, held its Bibles and hymnals, felt the heat of its candles.

—tasted the food on which the church sustains itself.

—sniffed the air across this broad country—from the Poconos, across the plains to the Cascades.

For the intuitive, we have

—gathered the hunches of its people as to what the church is really like.

—listened to wise men and women speculate on what may happen to the church.

—resonated to the hopes and dreams of the young, those in middle years, and the aged.

—searched within ourselves for our most competent analysis and our own intuitive sense of what the church might be like when it becomes what it seeks to be.

As one way to listen to the church and to give focus to our analysis, we utilized the Organizational Perception Indicator (OPI) as developed by The Management Design, Inc., Group (MDI), Cincinnati, Ohio.

Why Did We Choose the OPI?

The OPI measures perceptions of organizational *health.* We believe that a primary function of both leaders and administrators is to develop and maintain health and vitality in the organizations they serve. A look at the health of a conference is, then, a look at the effectiveness of its leaders and administrators.

The Population

For the survey, six conferences were chosen as representative, reflecting geographical distribution and variety in history, size, and style of leadership.

In each conference, the OPI was administered to people currently in formal leadership/administration positions, and also to a sample of laity and clergy not directly involved in current conference affairs. Altogether, approximately 1200 surveys were distributed and 857 were returned.

The OPI provides data on the following categories of perception:

G   *GOAL IDENTIFICATION* measures the way members see the goals of their conference. Are they realistic? Achievable? In touch with the basic identity of the group? Being acted upon?

R   *ROLE EXPECTATION* measures the degree of clarity members possess as to the expected functions of people in various positions in their conference.

L   *LEADERSHIP* scale registers members' evaluation of the present state of the leadership of the conference.

A   *ADMINISTRATION* measures follow-through, clarity of authority, accountability for decisions, and the extent to which direction and pacing of work is satisfactory. Every organization has a basic climate in which it "gets the job done."

C   *CONSONANCE* scale offers a picture of the degree to which members perceive that their conference lives out its expressed values. The method of behavior that puts order into the life of an organization can be more or less consistent with its deepest values.

P   *PROPONENCE* measures the degree to which the conference takes initiative in its work, rather than merely responding to each crisis it faces.

T   *TRANSCENDENCE* measures the degree to which the quality of life in the Christian community is perceived as exceeding normal human expectations.

D *DOUBT LEVEL* scale reflects the level of doubt that members may have about their conference. Decline in commitment is registered in increasing levels of doubt about the organization and its life.

The data gathered through the OPI has been integrated with other data gained through study of documents, direct observation of the church at work, and interviews with both individuals and groups. We believe the result fairly represents a broad perspective of the attitudes of United Methodists toward the leadership and administration of The United Methodist Church.

The summary perceptions, emergent questions, and models for the future are ours. We believe in them, own them, and are prepared to be held accountable for their content.

A Summary Report on the Survey

Explanation of Scales. The headings are the categories of perception included in the OPI survey. Numerically, the ratings can range from

a high of $+24$ = very positive perception, to

a low of -24 = very negative perception.

Note that a low reading in the doubt-level category means just that—*little doubt about the conference.* The average ratings of the total sample—655 men and 202 women—are shown in chart A, page 65. At first look, we see a pattern of generally lukewarm perceptions (in the $+5$ to $+10$ ranges), with only "transcendence" significantly higher. The average doubt level of approximately -2 tends to correlate, since we expect low doubt levels when the other categories are high. All in all, we see a mildly positive picture, with women consistently more positive than men about the overall health of the conferences of The United Methodist Church.

But, Let's Look Deeper. An average, as we well know, is just that—a quantity intermediate to a set of quantities. It gives a

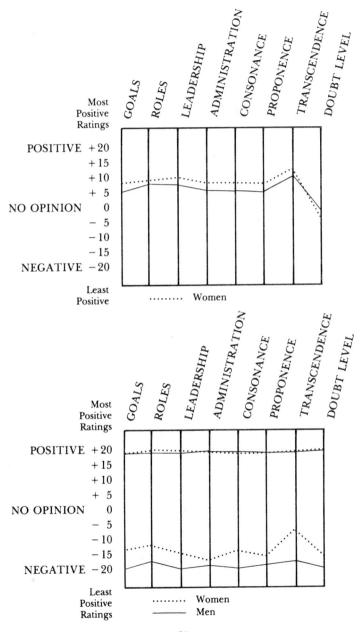

typical, homogenized picture—but we wondered if United Methodists really are as homogenized as all that!

We found that they are not! Let's look at the range in chart B, which shows the responses that were most positive (in the +20 range) and those that were least positive (from −15 to −20).

Worth noting in the chart: (a) Men and women tend to have top ratings (most positive) at about the same level; but (b) at the negative end of the scale, men rate the conferences much lower than do women. What might this indicate? Are women in the habit of expressing gentler opinions? Or do they expect less from the church and thus are less disappointed? Or do men desire something different from the church—something they are not receiving?

We would like to propose a hypothesis—a hypothesis based not on this data alone, but on the multitude of experiences we have had. We propose:

THAT THE UNITED METHODIST CHURCH HAS TENDED TO EMPHASIZE THE FEMININE AND FAMILY ASPECTS OF LIFE, TO THE PARTIAL EXCLUSION OF THE MASCULINE AND WORK SCENE (OTHER THAN HOMEMAKING).

Applied to conference life, one evidence of this was our sense that very few men, other than ordained ministers, play a significant role in conference life. It is an ordained- and female-dominated scene.

Proceeding, we found it enlightening to *sort* the survey data in various ways—to find the *patterns* of perceptions—and to extract from those patterns some additional hypotheses.

Let's Look at Some of Those Patterns. First of all, we will see if *age* is a significant factor.

The perception of "leadership" and "administration" in the church by those of differing ages presents a startling picture. There is high enthusiasm in young people up to age 25. Then the bottom drops out! From age 25 until 44, there seems to be a significant drop in positive perception.

Beginning at age 45, we see a gradual return to a more favorable stance, with people over 70 the most positive.

Now, let us look at just the laity—those who presently are members of Annual Conferences, and those who are not (at this time) These ratings show the average laity response for each OPI category.

	G	R	L	A	C	P	T	D
Present A/C	8.6	9.3	10.1	9.0	9.0	8.4	13.7	-3.5
Not A/C	7.0	7.2	8.2	6.3	7.6	6.2	12.5	-1.4

There is a consistent pattern indicating that those presently involved in an Annual Conference (its preparation, the meeting itself, and follow-up) are more positive about their conferences. Among the laity, then, let us propose this hypothesis:

THE MORE INVOLVED THE LAITY, THE MORE POSITIVE THEY ARE ABOUT THEIR CONFERENCE.

How About the Ordained Ministers? The survey dealt with four categories: members in full connection, associate members, probationary members, and special-appointment clergy. Look at the patterns of perception here:

	G	R	L	A	C	P	T	D
Full Connection	4.1	8.2	7.2	6.1	5.6	5.1	9.2	-0.6
Associate	3.0	8.6	1.3	4.3	5.3	7.3	10.6	2.0
Probationary	10.2	11.7	12.5	8.3	11 9	9.8	11.9	-7.8
Special Appointment	3.9	8.1	7.9	7.1	6.4	6.4	10.1	-1.0

Clear patterns would seem to be:
1. The ordained ministers are significantly less positive than the laity, with the exception of probationary members.
2. There is a lukewarm perception of the goals of the conferences, which implies an uncertain sense of direction.

3. There is least satisfaction with goals among special-appointment clergy (bishops, district superintendents, conference staff, seminary teachers, etc.)

Two very interesting hypotheses emerge:

THOSE PROFESSIONALLY INVOLVED IN THE CHURCH ARE MORE LIKELY THAN THE LAITY TO BECOME DISENCHANTED.

THE PROCESSES AND POLICIES BY WHICH THE UNITED METHODIST CHURCH DEVELOPS, SUPPORTS, AND PRO-MOTES ITS ORDAINED MINISTERS, TEND TO ALIENATE A SIGNIFICANT NUMBER.

Let's Explore That Possibility Further. Let's look specifically at the ratings of:

	G	R	L	A	C	P	T	D
Bishops	14.3	13.7	14.7	13.0	11.0	11.0	13.7	-14.3
Superintendents	8.0	11.4	12.3	10.6	8.7	8.4	12.9	-4.4

It would seem that these persons, all in positions of *governance* and *pastoral direction,* are very positive about their conferences. How does this compare with the ratings of those persons who are responsible for *program?*

	G	R	L	A	C	P	T	D
Council Directors	5.1	9.5	12.1	6.1	9.3	8.0	12.1	-3.3
Conference Program Staff	4.6	6.6	7.6	6.4	6.2	5.8	11.3	-0.4
District Program Staff	4.0	6.1	8.7	6.4	5.2	5.8	10.8	-1.5

The council directors and the program staff (both conference and district) generally show more "wear and tear" and are much less positive about the health of their conferences than are the bishops and district superintendents. Some other sorting gave us these patterns:

1. The conference lay leadership (the presidents of the women's groups, the presidents of the men's groups, the

lay leaders) tend to show high enthusiasm for their conferences. We would note, however, that while the presidents tend to rate the conferences consistently high, the lay leaders have a wide range of opinion—some to the point of strong alienation from conference leadership.

2. While the Council on Ministries chairpersons seem to be very favorable to the work of their conferences, *other chairpersons* do not seem to share this enthusiasm. While role perceptions seem to be clear, other aspects of conference life are less in tune.

3. Even more specifically, Council on Finance and Administration chairpersons seem to have questions about conference sense of direction (goals), competence in carrying out tasks (administration), and the degree to which beliefs are lived out (consonance).

Our hypothesis at this point takes us back to the fundamental paradox described in chapter 2.

THOSE IN POSITIONS OF LEADERSHIP (BISHOPS, DISTRICT SUPERINTENDENTS, LAY PRESIDENTS, LAY LEADERS) TEND TO REMAIN MORE POSITIVE ABOUT THE CHURCH THAN DO THOSE IN PROGRAM ADMINISTRATION (COUNCIL DIRECTORS, CONFERENCE STAFF, DISTRICT STAFF). CLEARLY, THE ADMINISTRATION OF PROGRAM, WORD, AND SYSTEM IS A MORE DRAINING ACTIVITY.

Some Reflections

Certainly it is good that the bishops and district superintendents seem to feel positive about their own leadership, and it is not really surprising that people with heavy program responsibility are less enthusiastic about the life of the conference. The work of program ministry, in itself, is demanding. In addition, the very nature of bureaucratic organizations (and certainly a United Methodist conference displays elements of bureaucracy) is such that continued work within the system inevitably builds in pressures that can lead to frustration and disenchantment.

While this phenomenon is not startling, it does produce a warning flag for the church. Suppose this pattern of disenchantment among the program staff not only continues, but grows—a normal pattern. We begin to see "burned out" staff—drained, empty of inspiration, increasingly negative, frustrated, and alienated from the church to which they have committed their lives. Some become ill; some drop out; others, usually with pastoral and psychological help, find a basis for renewed life. The pattern, then, suggests a significant challenge to the pastoral policies and procedures of the church:

1. Who is to carry out this special pastoral ministry?
2. What rhythms of life and work in the conference staff ministry will build in ongoing renewal, health-building patterns?

The future role of the laity in conference leadership seems to be both a major question and a major possibility. We will treat that matter later.

How About the Other Chairpersons? (that is, other than conference Council on Ministries chairpersons). The relative disaffection of dozens of "other" chairpersons seems to point to a waste of enormous potential. These are people who are obviously well thought of and highly committed to the conference. We assume they carry out their responsibilities—to a greater or lesser extent, of course. Yet the data would seem to indicate that they feel unappreciated, undervalued, and not in positions of legitimate influence. Probably this reaction is by no one's intent. The bishop, the cabinet, the council director—all recognize the value of these chairpersons and assume that they feel OK. But if they do not feel OK, a movement within the conference to include them, to overtly value the contribution they can and do make, will draw on immense potential for new vitality in the life of the conference. Hypothesis:

THE INTEGRATION OF ALL *CHAIRPERSONS INTO THE LIFE OF A CONFERENCE WOULD BE AN ENORMOUSLY PRODUCTIVE ACTIVITY.*

For example, the council director could meet regularly with *all the chairpersons as a team,* the primary agenda being to share and coordinate their efforts.

GOALS—A Special Concern

In all six conferences, a majority of those who responded to the OPI survey felt lukewarm about their goals and sense of direction. In addition, in every conference but one, there is a clearly defined segment which feels rather strongly that the sense of direction in their conference is not adequate. Either the direction is not clear, or they are in strong disagreement with the direction being taken.

Since perception about goals tends to give a quantitative measure of the vitality of an organization, the low rating on goals suggests a lack of energy—a dilution of commitment to the work of the conference. Indeed, considering the cluster of those opposed to the present directions, it seems a likelihood that considerable energy is being burned up in holding on to polarized positions or in carrying out political skirmishes.

Of further concern is the disparate perception of goals by the *governance group* (bishop, bishop's assistant, district superintendents) and by the *program staff* (both conference and district). Perhaps this is typical of the "burn-out" syndrome discussed previously. On the other hand, it may be that the processes of goal setting fail to coalesce the people of the conference into a common sense of direction.

It is our observation that goals that have to do with appointment making and budget development and apportionments, and also the goals of caucuses and of The United Methodist Women are clearer and apparently more achievable than programmatic goals. There seems to be general confusion and lack of information about programmatic concerns, combined with uneasiness about the relevance of many of them to congregational and world needs.

Goals related to the connectional system (election of General and Jurisdictional conference delegates) and to conference identity and structure are generally accepted, whereas programmatic concerns do not generate commitment. Hypothesis:

THE PEOPLE OF THE UNITED METHODIST CHURCH ARE CALLING FOR A NEW SENSE OF DIRECTION FROM THEIR LEADERS.

FURTHER, ANY NEW DIRECTIONAL GOALS MUST BE OF SUFFICIENT WORTH AND STATURE TO TRANSCEND THE LIMITED ADVOCACIES OF THE PRESENT.

Indeed, we are seriously concerned about the proliferation of single-issue advocacy stances. Despite the evident value of the separate causes, we believe it is producing widespread polarization which renders the church unable to act with vitality in a concerted fashion.

This polarization is further intensified by the current tendency toward the use of mathematical formulas to ensure representation. Such processes make it very difficult for representatives to function in a broad, for-the-good-of-the-whole manner.

TRANSCENDENCE—A Special Note

Essentially, this OPI rating scale is designed to measure the degree to which the quality of life in the Christian community transcends the blood, sweat, and tears that accompany the work of ministry. Is it all worthwhile? Is there a difference in our life together—a difference that is more than human effort can produce?

Consistently, the patterns in the study insist that this difference is present—that despite the wear and tear, the bickering and battles, the church continues to sense itself as God's people and that the Holy Spirit lives and moves among us.

Summary

In summary, let us rearrange our hypotheses and look at them again.

1. The United Methodist Church has tended to emphasize the feminine and family aspects of life, to the partial exclusion of the masculine and work scene (other than homemaking).

2. The more involved the laity, the more positive they are about their conference.

3. Those professionally involved in the church are more likely than the laity to become disenchanted.

4. The processes by which The United Methodist Church develops, promotes, and supports its ordained ministers tend to alienate a significant number.

5. Those in positions of *leadership* (bishops, district superintendents, lay presidents, lay leaders) tend to remain more positive about the church than do those in program *administration* (council directors, conference staff, district staff). Clearly, the administration of program, Word, and system is a draining activity.

6. The coordination of *all chairpersons* into the life of a conference would be an enormously productive activity.

7. The people of The United Methodist Church are calling for a new sense of direction from their leaders.

What's behind all this? In the next chapter we will look at some possible underlying causes.

CHAPTER 6

Some Basic Questions

Why Does the Historic Hesitancy
About Being a Church Continue?

Frederick A. Norwood, in *The Story of American Methodism,*
concluded the chapter "From Society to Church" with this
pungent sentence: "In some ways Methodists have not yet
decided whether to be a church or a society."

The history of duality is evident. In the beginning, John
Wesley was clear that his was no new church, but the
exhorting of people to band together in religious societies for
mutual encouragement. Church membership remained in
the Church of England, with its provision for normal Sunday
worship and the Sacraments.

This hesitancy about founding a new church was shared
also by the United Brethren and by the Evangelical
Association. As late as 1890, despite an active centralized
United Brethren church government, the emphasis was still
on being brethren—brothers in Christ—not a church *per se.*
The Evangelicals were clear about being an association, and
both groups were strongly affected by the pietist principle of
the little church within the church.

So it would seem that the tensions of Spirit and order of the
first-century church remain writ large on the forming
processes of those who now call themselves United Methodists.
The paradoxical balancing-out of a Spirit-filled existence,
within a framework of order and discipline, will continue to be

a primary challenge to The United Methodist Church as it enters its third century.

An Example of Continued Hesitancy. Perhaps the church's reluctance to embrace symbols of unity is an extension of this historic hesitancy. For example:

—There is no *one national location* that might be called the headquarters of The United Methodist Church.

—There is no *one council* at any level of the church that can speak with authority. It always must exist in a check-and-balance situation—that is, the Council on Ministries vis-à-vis the Council on Finance and Administration vis-à-vis the Council of Bishops.

—The Council of Bishops has no symbolic head, other than the temporary president.

—The emphasis is on bishops and district superintendents as administrators, rather than as symbolic leaders of the church in their areas. Indeed, the current processes of nomination and election of the episcopacy do not appear to us to put first priority on demonstrated leadership ability. The functional paradigm of bishops as managers of conferences and of the episcopacy as a board of managers of the denomination tends to call for administrative skills, rather than the charismatic qualities of leadership.

—Liturgically, there is a lack of emphasis on the Holy Communion, a traditional symbol of unity within the Church. John Wesley, of course, issued instructions to his preachers to devise forms of worship that were not in competition with the forms of the Church of England. But he expected everyone to participate in the normal Sunday celebration of the Eucharist.

Why Today? A primary function of leadership is to coalesce unity within a designated group of people. It seems appropriate to raise this question:

COULD THE UNITED METHODIST CHURCH BECOME MORE TRULY UNIFIED BY MAKING USE OF SYMBOLS AND RITUALS WHICH DRAMATIZE THE UNITY IT SEEKS?

We propose that the "re-formation" and renewal of both leadership and administration in the conference have to do with interaction with the Word and the Sacraments, not simply in a mechanical or formal sense, but also in a liturgical and personal way. The transcendent reality of Christ and the presence of the Holy Spirit through the Word and in the Sacrament make direct contribution to the discovery of new life and order. Indeed, understanding leadership and administration as gifts of the Spirit is essential to their contribution to the Body of Christ.

What Is to Be the Role of the Laity in the Leadership and Administration of The United Methodist Church?

In looking at history, we find that the people called United Methodist never have been quite sure where the laity fits into the scheme of things. In a grammatical sense, the question might be posed, Is the laity the *subject* or the *object* of ministry? Put another way, Is the primary ministry of the Church the work of the ordained only, or of all baptized Christians? It is interesting to reflect on the perception of the developing role of clergy vis–à-vis that of laity during the past fifty years in the United States.

It is obvious that over the years, we have increased our expectations of the paid clergy's service to the church. It seems obvious also that the clergy have accepted these expectations as reasonable. Pastors are responsible people, and there is more and more to be responsible for! Never mind that it becomes an intolerable load; never mind that it robs the lay people of their proper ministry to church and world! The pattern certainly reinforces the pictures of the church as a clergy union, filled with those skilled in special trades—trades not open to the people they serve.

Then There Is a Governance Question. Questions about the laity have smouldered for a long time. Since Wesley perceived himself as coalescing a band of itinerant preachers, rather than as founding a church, the laity has had a place in the scheme of things—to be lay pastors, to form the religious societies and to exhort them to greater fervor. Yet the local lay pastor was clearly a third-class citizen in governance questions.

And so it continued. The itinerant preacher was the fair-haired boy of the Methodist system. Annual Conferences, by definition, were annual gatherings of itinerant preachers. Only after a hundred years did lay representation begin to be accepted—by the Methodist Episcopal Church, South, in 1854; in 1872, in the north (but to General Conference only); and finally in 1932, lay participation in the Annual Conference was assured.

But is it really assured now? To quote one of our interviewees, "There is strong evidence that generally the laity is used and ignored, praised and humiliated by the clergy, who wish to generate lay enthusiasm for clerically conceived programs and fund allocation."

Who makes up The United Methodist Church? What are their functions? These are questions that have haunted the church for a long time. As it looks into its third century, the questions still remain.

We believe that the laity is a source of great latent energy for The United Methodist Church. Further, it seems probable that this energy could be released by such means as: (a) more involvement in setting directions for the conference; (b) more involvement in the governance process itself; (c) more involvement in works of ministry in the conference, in the district, and in the local church.

The release of this fountain of energy may require a radical shift of stance for some pastors. The ministry of the laity—the nonordained—is not to be exercised primarily within the walls and functions of the local church (or district, or conference). The primary arena is and must be the *world*—the day-to-day ministry of a Christian who is also a teacher, an electrician, or a farmer.

Certainly the local church is a community that gathers for worship and mutual support. But it also must gather to train—"to equip the saints for the work of ministry." The role of the pastor as trainer, as equipper of the laity for the ministry in the world, is crucial. As the pastor can shift his or her focus to this role, so will the witness of the laity be enhanced.

Here are some specific shapes that this training/equipping might take:

—parish study groups on the ministry of the church in the world;

—weekday luncheon vocational groups to discuss the special witness of Christians who are attorneys, firemen, department store executives, mothers;

—visits by the pastor to the places where his or her people work;

—leadership-skill training, for both members and non-members of the church, to enhance the leadership of the whole civic community (e.g., How about sessions for city council members?).

Obviously, the role of the conference is to provide trainers of trainers—to seek out, recruit, and train those who can work directly with the laity. This is not to suggest that all trainers/equippers ought to be clergy. Here is a clear and appropriate role for laity, too. Indeed, some of our laity have immense skill and experience in training and equipping others—skill and experience that probably is available to the church, if asked for. Perhaps this is an area where the laity must assume leadership if it is to happen!

Is There a Historic, Competitive "I Win—You Lose" Mentality in The United Methodist Church?

Certainly the initial period of the formation of John Wesley's societies was one of struggle and conflict—conflict with the established Church of England, with political interests, with mob prejudice and violence. Our visions of the preaching bands, rescuing people "from the wrath to come," have a real sense of competition.

In the American colonies, the political consequences of the Great Awakening prepared the soil for the Revolutionary War. The war itself and the struggles for dominance that followed were the environment in which the Methodist movement shaped its own sense of identity. The image of the itinerant preacher, charging across the Alleghenies into the Ohio Country—into a hostile land—was a part of the strategy of an army fighting for Christ against the world, the flesh, and the devil.

Thus there is a strong precedent for viewing the church as being in an *adversary stance* against society, with a clear goal of winning—of overcoming the enemy. One can make a case that in the early days, perhaps even during the first hundred years of the Methodist movement, that stance proved very helpful in building a sense of unity in the young church. Political leaders have long known that rallying their people against a common enemy is a very effective tool for coalescing support (cf. W. R. Bion and his "fight/flight" group).[1] John Wesley's strategies and those of Francis Asbury proved no less effective.

What might be seen today as the organizational conse-quences of this adversary stance—this strategy? First of all, there seems to be a tendency to look upon the clergy as troops sent into battle, to die if necessary! Losses are expected. Most circuit riders died by age 40! With the poor history of battlefield medicine, there may be an inherited tendency to replace, rather than to repair the warriors. A present-day phenomenon that might be linked to this stance is the tendency toward size—large quantities of clergy; large groups as a norm. Also, it is our perception that there is a lack of systemic concern for the re-creation, the renewal, of the clergy. Individual bishops and individual district superintendents show immense pastoral concern for their clergy folk, but conference policies and procedures seem woefully lacking.

A second consequence of this stance may be the tendency toward political, rather than consensual models of church government. As we pointed out earlier, Asbury felt that representation and democratic sentiments were not suitable for a spiritual church government: For an army fighting a common enemy, democratic governance clearly is less effective. But as American church life has moved through its second century, the common enemy has become less visible. The church is less under open attack; the "enemy" has become diffuse. Indeed, there are many who would take a Pogo stance—"We have met the enemy and they are us!"

Perhaps it is a natural progression: A group will search around for internal enemies when the outside enemy becomes less apparent. At any rate, there is evidence in our study that the Annual Conference meeting has become a battleground—or at least a jousting arena! Political strategies are developed; coalitions are formed; the most persuasive speakers are recruited to present our views—all to provide an arena for our special interest *to win!*

The spoils of war go to those who are most successful in putting votes together—or perhaps to those who are most skilled in the manipulation of *Robert's Rules of Order.* The established use of *Robert's Rules* is in itself indicative of the inherited adversary stance, since (in our perception) it is an excellent set of rules for a political war game!

But where there are winners, there also are losers. During our observations at Annual Conference meetings, there was a fair number of bloodied people, of walking wounded. But perhaps the most wounded of all are the hundreds of sincere members of Annual Conferences who come . . . and watch the knights of political manuever play their games. Later, we will propose a different model for Annual Conference gatherings—a model more participative in nature and more collegial in its approach to church governance.

The image of an army of preachers is clearly in tension with later governance developments, both in secular society and in the church ecumenical. It is also in tension with the biblical image of the church as redemptive community—as peaceable kingdom. Perhaps the drive to win is innate. There are clearly many within the church who derive great enjoyment from the struggles and fencing at Annual Conference—"The adrenalin flows, it's exciting, it's fun. It's my gift!"

Is there a balance to be found between Spirit and order—between battle and peace? We think so—and we believe the finding of this balance is of major importance for The United Methodist Church and for its leaders.

Are UMC Leaders Presiding Over a Church in Which the Basic Energy Flow Is Constricted?

St. Paul's analogy between the church and the human body is extraordinarily useful in examining the state of the church. Just as the body, with its many parts, is yet one, so it is with the church and the many entities that cause it to function. Just as the body can be in a state of either disease or exuberant health, so can the church.

A key way to assess the health of the body is to examine its circulatory system—the heart, arteries and veins, and blood pressure and flow. Equally valid in assessing the vitality of the church is the examination of the flow of its lifeblood—the flow of power and energy in the system.

In the New Testament, "power" is an appropriate word. Indeed, Acts and the Epistles tell a story of empowerment— the way in which God, through the Holy Spirit, entered into the young church and gave it life, energy, and direction. Throughout the centuries, churches have endeavored to maintain this Spirit-filled, empowered life.

Power in church governance is exhibited through the responsible performance of four basic roles:
—*evaluator* of life and ministry
—*recommender* of future directions
—*decider* of directions
—*action-taker* in tasks of ministry

By assessing the way these roles are established and distributed, and the degree to which their responsibilities are carried out, one can readily tell how well a church's lifeblood is flowing.

In this study of The United Methodist Church, certain symptoms of restricted flow have appeared (a bit of arteriosclerosis, to play out the analogy). We have listed some of them here.

Size. The sheer size of conferences, the numbers of churches and clergy, and the size of Annual Conference meetings contribute to the present problems in conference leadership and administration and thus seriously reduce the vitality (flow of energy) of the church.

Functional Incoherence. The inherited design for the leadership and administration of the conference by bishop, district superintendents, conference staff, and elected and appointed laity and clergy who serve a multitude of boards and agencies, is a functional swamp, filled with quicksand that generally suffocates creativity and saps energy. Certainly it is highly desirable that both clergy and laity have significant involvement in the life of the conference, but the present arrangement seems lacking in *coherence.* Farther on, we will propose a more coherent arrangement.

Purpose of the Annual Conference Meeting. The absence of any Disciplinary objectives for the Annual Conference meeting contributes to a lack of clarity and direction. Fundamentally a gathering of preachers, it has become a bureaucratic nightmare, managed by people of great goodwill whose efforts are diminished by lack of trust, idolization of discussion, and the use of the conference as a sphere of influence by persons who believe themselves unfairly disempowered. Indeed, the use of the Annual Conference meeting as a forum by special-interest groups, which are attempting to achieve recognition by
  —obtaining special attention, even if disruptive
  —requesting new or additional budget allocations
  —attracting supporters

suggests that many believe they do not receive fair treatment in the ongoing processes of the conference. Certainly the conference floor is *one* place to achieve redress of grievances, but the number of groups that use this strategy seems to indicate that they find the ongoing processes controlled by others with whom they have little influence.

The very agenda of the meeting seems to be a classic example of progressive redirection. From the initial gatherings of itinerant preachers to discuss the work, pray together, and receive reassignment, the Annual Conference has accumulated many trappings of legislative bureaucracy. Multitudinous reports and much budget tinkering (most decisions already have been made elsewhere) tend to portray the Annual Conference's main function as legislative. Yet, its very size—several hundred to well over 2000—renders it almost unworkable for significant involvement of the delegates in serious discussion. In short, the group is too large, and the items for discussion are too small to achieve effective legislation.

As a gathering of the church to celebrate, to honor, to witness together, to shape broad directions, to laugh and to cry, the Annual Conference has immense potential. The vehicle is there—but it calls out for a new (or very old) approach.

Restrictive Budgeting. One prime way to restrict the life flow of an organization is through institutionalized budgeting. By this we mean the tendency to build in *ongoing* budgetary allocations. Once built in, many of these items never come up for review; they become part of the so-called fixed expenses. We would propose that in a truly healthy fiscal system, there are *no fixed expenses*—that, at the strategic level, all major items need regular evaluation to determine if they still move the church in the direction it has chosen.

Programs have outlived their usefulness; buildings no longer support the works of ministry; boards, committees, and commissions become more engrossed with their own perpetuation than with serving their original purpose. *All this we know.* Yet far too few conference budgetary processes reflect a *conscious coordination of budgets with the goals to be achieved.*

We propose that the Annual Conferences, if they have not already done so, proceed with processes to articulate clear goals and directions for the years ahead; and having articulated those goals, that they deliberately and intentionally allocate resources of people, buildings, equipment, and money to their achievement. This sense of intentionality (e.g., In what way and to what degree does this program lead to the achievement of specific conference goals?) provides a base for the better superintending of programs and projects. Accountability will be enhanced and the opportunity to *celebrate* achievements of ministry will be honestly provided. In addition, clear goals *attract resources!* More energy, more Spirit-filled vitality, will be at work in the challenging ministries demanded by the decade of the 80s.

Now some will say, "We already have goals—and nothing much happens." Others will say, "That's just Management by Objectives, which hasn't demonstrated that it is truly effective." We reply in this way:

If—the goals are *worthy of the mission* of the church;

If—the *people* have *participated* responsibly in the *setting* of goals;

If—the goals are *translated into creative activities* that enable their achievement;

If—the *broad allocation of resources* is tied visibly to these goals in conference *budget*—

then, in our experience, new life comes and resources multiply as needed to do the work, just as they did in the story of Jesus and the feeding of the multitude.

As to Management by Objectives, it is a useful technique and one that could be quite useful for conference staffs. It is not, however, a substitute for the setting of clear goals for the work of the conference. Indeed, the evaluation of direction is a *primary task* of leadership in the church—a leadership that includes Annual Conference lay and clergy members and bishops alike! If, then, these questions are operative:

—hesitancy at being a church?
—the role of the laity?
—our historic militancy?
—restricted energy flow? . . .

What Might We Do to Change the Situation?

We, with appropriate fear and trembling, propose the following: (1) *a model for leadership and administration in The United Methodist Church,* and (2) *some specific recommendations for action.*

CHAPTER 7

A Model for Leadership and Administration in a Coherent, Connectional, Conference

What do we mean by a coherent, connectional, conference? "Coherent" is defined as united, connected naturally or logically; *The Discipline* states the connectional principle that "All United Methodists and United Methodist congregations are connected in a network of conciliar and legal relationships."

It is clear that to be coherent and to be connectional is to be in relationship. But what sort of relationship? Both people and congregations can be in natural and logical relationships. In addition, they can be in dependent, independent, or *inter*dependent relationships. To explore these particular relationships, let us look at a natural growth pattern.

In the beginning, as children, we are all in a dependent relationship.

DEPENDENT ⟶ **PARENTS**

**childlike
immature**

As we grow and reach our teen years, we exhibit signs of independence, rejecting our dependency on our parents. Sometimes this rejection can take violent forms. True independence requires separation—a distancing of ourselves from our parents. Some of us never get beyond that point;

we separate ourselves, become alien to our family, and never enter into relationship again.

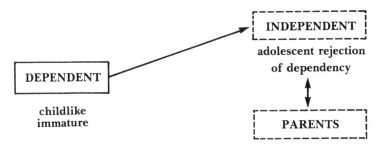

How can we move beyond that point . . . to a relationship we can call interdependent? Doing so requires, first, authentic independence—a true separation from the childlike, immature relationship. And it also requires the same authentic independence on the part of the parents—they must be fully independent as themselves. So as independence is truly achieved, interdependence—the mature relating of independent beings—becomes possible.

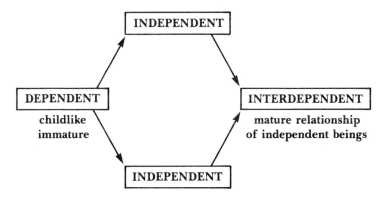

Now, how does this growth pattern apply to *connection* in The United Methodist Church? If *connection* is to be vital, it must reflect an interdependent relationship, and it must be a life-giving experience for the people and the organizational

entities that make up the church. Operationally, this calls for
two principles:

1. Persons and organizational entities must have clear,
   unambiguous identity and autonomy in appropriate
   areas of life and work.
2. Persons and entities must have clear, authentic channels
   for relating *to* each other.

In other words, the degree to which the people and the entities
of the church are, at the same time, both FREE and RELATED,
correlates directly with the strength and vitality of the church.
Just as *Spirit* and *Word* must be held in paradoxical tension, so
must *freedom* and *order*. To this end, we propose:

*A MODEL FOR LEADERSHIP AND ADMINISTRATION IN A
COHERENT, CONNECTIONAL, CONFERENCE OF THE
UNITED METHODIST CHURCH.*

*The First Part of the Model Deals with **Flow**.* The currents of life
and energy in the church do not flow in a straight line—a
constant pattern—but tend to follow cycles, in which the energy
rises, then declines, then is renewed. Indeed, the basic ongoing
process of life, death, and resurrection is the continuing
experience of the church, both in the first century and today.

So it is with a coherent, connectional conference. There are
times when the energy of the conference is growing rapidly—
especially in terms of a particular goal or mission to be achieved.

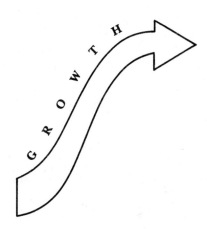

These are followed by times when the energy declines, used up in the work of ministry. Just as particular goals coalesce energy, the carrying out of specific programs consumes the energy produced.

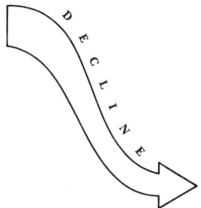

After the period of decline runs its course, there is a time of resurgence—of renewal. . . .

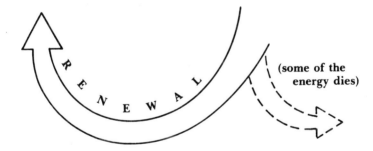

If we connect these phases, we get this sort of pattern:

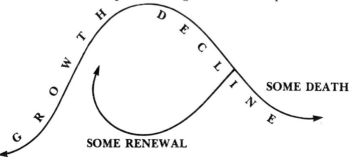

Now, how do the elements that make up a conference fit into this pattern of life flow? Let us take a graphic look at the model.

THE MODEL CONTAINS THESE BUILDING BLOCKS

1	THE SUPPORTIVE MEMBERSHIP
2	THE ANNUAL CONFERENCE MEETING
3	CONFERENCE COUNCIL
4	THE BISHOP AS LEADER
5	THE BISHOP AS ADMINISTRATOR
6a	THE COUNCIL DIRECTOR AS PROGRAM DIRECTOR

and

6b	THE STAFF (CONFERENCE AND DISTRICT)
7	THE DISTRICT SUPERINTENDENTS
8	PARTICIPANTS IN THE PROCESS OF MINISTRY
9	RECIPIENTS OF MINISTRY
10	THOSE WHO MIGHT ADVISE

THESE BUILDING BLOCKS ARE ARRANGED IN A SPECIAL WAY

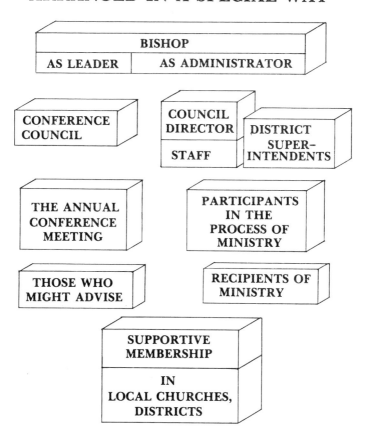

Why are the blocks arranged in this manner? What sort of special relationships and special functions are implied? Let us again diagram the flow of energy—the vital life processes—in the model (page 93).

The model is based upon several principles, which we now apply to the Annual Conference of The United Methodist Church.

1. THE SUPPORTIVE MEMBERSHIP

THROUGH THEIR BAPTISM, ALL CHRISTIANS ARE CALLED TO MEMBERSHIP AND MINISTRY IN THE CHURCH, AND THEREFORE TO RESPONSIBLE PARTICIPATION IN ITS LIFE.

This participation should include the ongoing worship and other activities of the local congregation. All are called to be *givers*—to provide the resources of money, time, ideas, and presence needed to nurture the life of the Christian community. All are called to be *receivers*—to receive the gifts of the Spirit and the gifts of service offered by others.

As a selected group, some are called to be members of Annual Conference—a calling to special leadership in The United Methodist Church, as either lay or ordained ministers.

All are part of the supportive membership of the church and as such, they carry on an ongoing dialogue with the Annual Conference (page 94).

2. THE ANNUAL CONFERENCE MEETING

THIS CALLING TO LEADERSHIP IN THE ANNUAL CONFERENCE, AN EXPRESSION OF THE HOLY SPIRIT, AWAKENS ENORMOUS ENERGY LATENT IN THE CHURCH.

A prime function of the Annual Conference is to provide a locus and forum for this leadership—to tap the

THE FLOW OF POWER
IN THE CHURCH

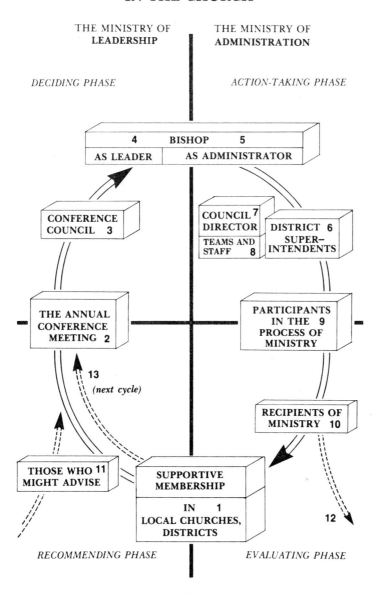

THE MINISTRY OF
LEADERSHIP

THE MINISTRY OF
ADMINISTRATION

DECIDING PHASE

ACTION-TAKING PHASE

4   BISHOP   5

AS LEADER | **AS ADMINISTRATOR**

**CONFERENCE
COUNCIL   3**

**COUNCIL 7
DIRECTOR**

**TEAMS AND
STAFF   8**

**DISTRICT 6
SUPER–
INTENDENTS**

**THE ANNUAL
CONFERENCE
MEETING 2**

**PARTICIPANTS
IN THE 9
PROCESS OF
MINISTRY**

13
(next cycle)

**RECIPIENTS OF
MINISTRY 10**

**THOSE WHO 11
MIGHT ADVISE**

**SUPPORTIVE
MEMBERSHIP**

**IN   1
LOCAL CHURCHES,
DISTRICTS**

12

RECOMMENDING PHASE

EVALUATING PHASE

93

THE ONGOING DIALOGUE BETWEEN:

THE SUPPORTIVE ◄—*and*————► THE
MEMBERSHIP   ANNUAL CONFERENCE
(in the Local Churches)   (through its Members)
(in the District Meetings)

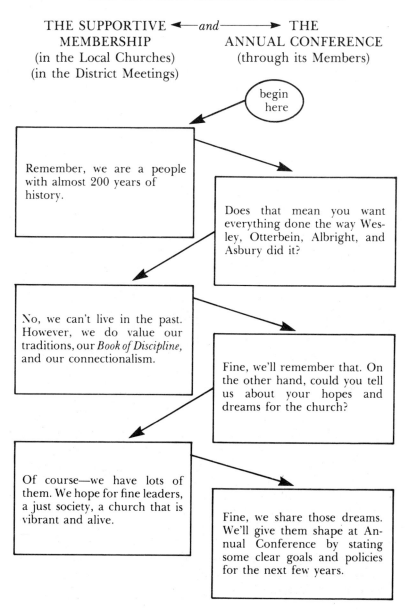

begin here

Remember, we are a people with almost 200 years of history.

Does that mean you want everything done the way Wesley, Otterbein, Albright, and Asbury did it?

No, we can't live in the past. However, we do value our traditions, our *Book of Discipline,* and our connectionalism.

Fine, we'll remember that. On the other hand, could you tell us about your hopes and dreams for the church?

Of course—we have lots of them. We hope for fine leaders, a just society, a church that is vibrant and alive.

Fine, we share those dreams. We'll give them shape at Annual Conference by stating some clear goals and policies for the next few years.

energy by giving it focus and direction. How can this be accomplished? We propose the following strategies:

A. That the conference stay in touch with its heritage, a source of energy, and again include the three historic topics of early conferences as primary agenda items:
—the mission of the church
—ways to carry out this mission
—how to live together as Christians;

B. That it maintain its connectional nature, both by its rituals of assignment of the ordained ministry and by an ongoing search for appropriate contemporary expressions of itineracy;

C. That it act out the historic rituals of preaching, small-group Bible study, and discussion, in order to maintain its sense of continuing identity;

D. That it capture the dreams and visions of its people by focusing its legislative agenda on broad *goals* and *policies* and eliminating the present emphasis on dozens of minute program items;

E. That it celebrate the achievement of its goals and of its people, honor them, and give thanks to God;

F. That it lay to rest (with appropriate grieving) programs that no longer produce life and renewal. By this we mean the deliberate and regular cessation of programs and the elimination of structural units no longer needed.

Since the gathering of Annual Conference itself must reflect the paradoxical tension between Spirit-filled freedom and disciplined order, we propose an intentional duality in makeup.

First, we would increase the size of Annual Conference sessions. If we are to witness to the exuberance of the Spirit in great services of celebration and preaching, we must have as much of the body there as possible—plus radio and television coverage. If we can gather 50,000 people for a football game, why not for the church? If we have something important to say, let us proclaim it boldly!

On the other hand, we would reduce the number of persons entrusted with legislative choices to a more effective number (perhaps 200 to 300). It was very clear in our observations of Annual Conferences that most of the members are effectively silenced; they are hesitant to speak in front of so large a body. The vocal few who are experienced and skillful in the machinations of Annual Conference usually receive the limelight and get their way.

If we are to have true discipline and coherent legislation, rooted in prayerful, intelligent discussion, we must entrust a body of leaders to act responsibly in our behalf.

AN ANNUAL CONFERENCE MEETING BASED ON THOSE PRINCIPLES MIGHT LOOK LIKE THIS:

○ Daily sessions of small groups for prayer, Bible study, and discussion.

○ Visioning sessions that lead to the articulation of broad, achievable goals for the conference.

○ Two or three major policy questions (such as "clergy renewal" or "ministry of the laity"), which have been developed extensively in prior district sessions. In all cases, alternative proposals have been formulated, and Annual Conference chooses from among them.

○ A consensual method of decision on goals and policies, rather than the use of *Robert's Rules of Order*. Consensual modes do much to build unity in the church and to reduce the hard feelings brought about by political methods. Perhaps we can sponsor debates and preaching competitions for those whose makeup requires competition.

3. THE CONFERENCE COUNCIL

ONGOING COHERENCE IS PROVIDED BY A BODY OF TRUST-HOLDERS, OR (to use more traditional United Methodist nomenclature) A CONFERENCE COUNCIL, ELECTED BY ANNUAL CONFERENCE,

AND *ENTRUSTED WITH POWER TO ACT* ON BE-
HALF OF THE CONFERENCE BETWEEN ANNUAL
MEETINGS.

As much as we expect the Annual Conference to act
wisely and to make responsible choices, it is difficult, in a
few days once a year, to bring everything to a high level of
specificity. Nor is it desirable!

If the Annual Conference spells out *only broad goals and
policies,* and if there is *nobody* to *translate* these into specific
guidelines and actions—*we produce confusion* in the church.
The leadership of the Annual Conference has spoken—
but nothing happens!

On the other hand, if the Annual Conference goes into
great detail in its legislation, designating specific program
budgets (or even personnel selection!), it wears itself out.
Much legislation is postponed until the last minute; hasty
decisions are made; tempers flare; key matters simply are
not dealt with. Therefore, if the church is to be *coherent*
and truly *connectional,* Annual Conference must empower
an ongoing council to act in its behalf between meetings.
The nature of their ongoing dialogue is illustrated on
page 100.

FUNCTIONS OF THE CONFERENCE COUNCIL

PRIMARY FUNCTIONS	EXPRESSED IN THESE WAYS
A. To maintain a *sense of direction* for the conference, congruent with the expressed desires of the Annual Conference and the general membership.	○ The goals and personnel designated by the Annual Conference are made more specific: —goals translated into specific, timed objectives

—personnel choices made and people called
—new or modified directions identified and developed.

B. To maintain a *quality of life* and performance consistent with the beliefs and heritage of the conference.

○ Broad policies enunciated by the Annual Conference are translated into guidelines and procedures.
○ New or modified policy needs are identified and developed.
○ Progress toward stated goals is monitored.
○ Elected personnel are supported by:
—clear role descriptions
—clear expectations regarding standards of performance
—resources adequate to achieve expectations
—adequate compensation
—adequate working conditions.

C. To insure the healthy functioning of the major systemic elements of the conference through ongoing monitoring.

○ In order to maintain a systemic overview, the council must be knowledgeable about (but not involved in) the workings of the ministry teams, preparation for Annual Conferences, and the thinking of the general membership. Therefore it is crucial that the council receive intelligent, timely reports from these areas, with special emphasis on emerging goal and policy questions.
○ The council reports on its *own* performance and stewardship to the Annual Conference and membership.
○ The council reports on the performance of major sys-

temic elements of the conference to the Annual Conference and membership.

D. To mobilize and allocate sufficient resources, people, objects, and money for the works of ministry.

○ *Mobilization:*
—ongoing assessment of degree of mobilization of present and potential resources
—development of strategies to mobilize potential resources
—monitoring balance of needed resources and supply

○ *Allocation:*
—development of system of priorities
—development of alternative budgets for submission to council

THE BISHOP
4. AS LEADER AND
5. AS ADMINISTRATOR

AS IN THE EARLY CHURCH, THERE IS A HISTORIC TENSION IN THE UNITED METHODIST CHURCH BETWEEN SPIRIT AND OFFICE—BETWEEN SPIRITUAL POWER AND LEGAL AUTHORITY.

This dialectic relationship between the vitality of Spirit and the authority of office shapes the very nature, the essence, of the role of chief leader (bishop) and chief administrator (general superintendent).

Essentially, the bishop must embody both roles of the tension—*as leader,* to facilitate processes by which the power of the Spirit is released within the people; *as*

THE ONGOING DIALOGUE BETWEEN:

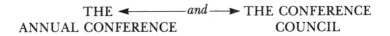

THE ANNUAL CONFERENCE ◄——— *and* ——► THE CONFERENCE COUNCIL

begin
here

Speaking for our people, we wish to achieve these goals for the conference in the next five years.

Those goals are pretty broad. We've made them more specific and separated them into objectives. O.K.? Also, do you have other guidance for us?

We like the way you've sharpened the goals. Our other guidance would be to keep these basic UMC principles in mind.

Fine, that's really helpful. We're asking our staff and other program people to devise strategies to achieve the goals/objectives.

To help provide direction, we charge the bishop with responsibility for oversight of the whole conference.

We will respect him and work with him. We'll report our progress to you next year.

administrator, to direct authoritatively the processes by which the church carries out its tasks of ministry; and finally, to preside over the rituals through which the anxieties produced by this tension are reduced.

Perhaps it would be helpful to outline the way in which the two roles (bishop/general superintendent) are carried out.

FUNCTIONS OF THE BISHOP

PRIMARY FUNCTIONS	EXPRESSED IN THESE WAYS
A. As bishop— To *lead* the conference, to call it forth to ministry, to hold in front of all the people a vision of the work and mission of the church	○ Integrate into his or her own person: —an attention and obedience to the Word of God as it is received in the Scriptures, in the Church at large, and in the local faith community —an ability and discipline to engage in solitary prayer and communal worship —a sensitivity to the concerns, needs, and hopes of the conference and of the entire society. ○ Accept the historic role of prophet, speaking to and for the church, boldly and with conviction. ○ Embody the role of symbolic leader—that person who symbolizes the unity we seek, without apology or false humility. ○ Coordinate the development flow of goals and policy —by insuring that the new learnings, hopes, and

questions that emerge from the people and from the tasks of ministry are fed into appropriate bodies. (Specifically, that goal/policy implications/recommendations developed by the ministry teams or task forces are communicated to the conference council.)

○ Maintain a bonding process among members of the church through local church visits, district and conference meetings, and ceremonial occasions.

B. As general superintendent—To *administer* the work of the church; to direct and support the *tasks of ministry* among the people

○ Delegate pastoral oversight for the districts to the district superintendents.

○ Delegate responsibility and authority for conference program to the council director.

The bishop, to be in true connection, must carry on dialogue with several groups and persons. Most especially, he or she maintains connection with the conference council, the district superintendents, and the council director. First let us illustrate the dialogue with the conference council (page 103).

6. DISTRICT SUPERINTENDENTS

This delegation emerges initially from the human desire for order—for *place* within the structure—on the part of the ordained ministry. That normal desire calls for an appropriate response from the conference—the provision of areas, or districts, in which peer relationship and superintendency can be exercised. The connectional nature of this relationship is illustrated on page 104.

THE ONGOING DIALOGUE BETWEEN:

THE ←———— *and* ———→ THE BISHOP
CONFERENCE COUNCIL   (as Leader/Administrator)

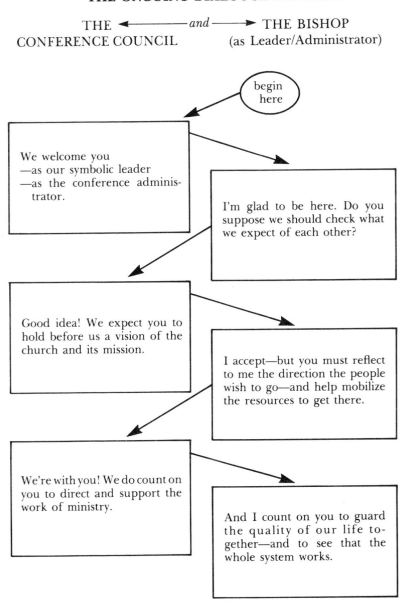

begin
here

We welcome you
—as our symbolic leader
—as the conference administrator.

I'm glad to be here. Do you
suppose we should check what
we expect of each other?

Good idea! We expect you to
hold before us a vision of the
church and its mission.

I accept—but you must reflect
to me the direction the people
wish to go—and help mobilize
the resources to get there.

We're with you! We do count on
you to direct and support the
work of ministry.

And I count on you to guard
the quality of our life together—and to see that the
whole system works.

103

THE ONGOING DIALOGUE BETWEEN:

THE BISHOP ◄——— *and* ———► THE DISTRICT
(as General Superintendent)　　　　　　SUPERINTENDENTS

(begin here)

I appreciate your willingness to share with me in this heavy task of being shepherd to this conference.

We share the load with you gladly and commit ourselves to pastoral concern for all the people.

All the people includes supporting each other in trying situations.

But it also means participating in the joyful celebrations of the church.

Together, we will carry out the public ministry of the conference to the world around us.

We convenant with you to carry out our responsibilities faithfully, so help us God!

7. THE COUNCIL DIRECTOR

The council director is to coordinate the work of the church in cooperation with the Conference Council (illustrated on pages 106 and 107). Specifically, he or she is to:

A. Select and appoint competent staff, with appropriate training for each specific job;

B. Enable (through delegation) the staff to organize their particular ministries in such a way that the goals and objectives of the conference are met;

C. Convene and coordinate the particular ministries, to assure healthy interaction among them;

D. Maintain accountability:
  —help staff evaluate their work
  —relate work of teams to the mission of the church
  —report progress, or lack of it, to the conference council;

E. Develop and install improved methods of program ministry;

F. Thank people and provide appropriate celebrations!

8. TEAMS AND STAFF

THE TEAMS

IN ORDER TO ASSURE CONTINUING COHERENCE IN THE WORK OF THE CONFERENCE, THERE MUST BE TEAMWORK AMONG THE PEOPLE RESPONSIBLE FOR THE WORK, AND COORDINATION AMONG THE TEAMS.

Essentially, it seems that three primary teams should exist in the ongoing life of a conference:

A. *THE CONFERENCE MINISTRY TEAM*

The Conference Ministry Team consists of the bishop, the district superintendents, the council director, and the staff (the directors of the goal task forces).

THE ONGOING DIALOGUE BETWEEN:

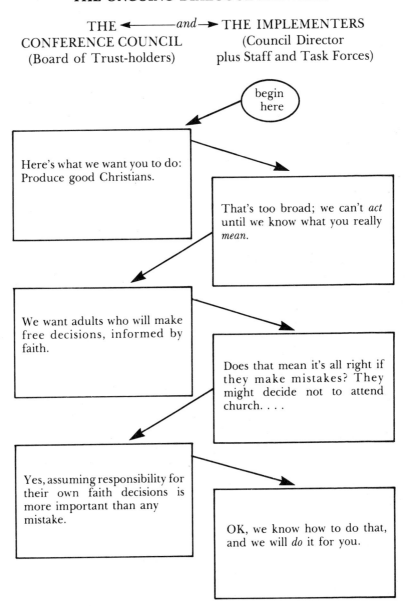

THE ←———and→ THE IMPLEMENTERS
CONFERENCE COUNCIL   (Council Director
(Board of Trust-holders)   plus Staff and Task Forces)

begin
here

Here's what we want you to do:
Produce good Christians.

That's too broad; we can't *act*
until we know what you really
mean.

We want adults who will make
free decisions, informed by
faith.

Does that mean it's all right if
they make mistakes? They
might decide not to attend
church. . . .

Yes, assuming responsibility for
their own faith decisions is
more important than any
mistake.

OK, we know how to do that,
and we will *do* it for you.

A SECOND DIALOGUE

THE ◄——— *and* ———► THE IMPLEMENTERS
CONFERENCE COUNCIL   (Council Director
plus Staff and Task Forces)

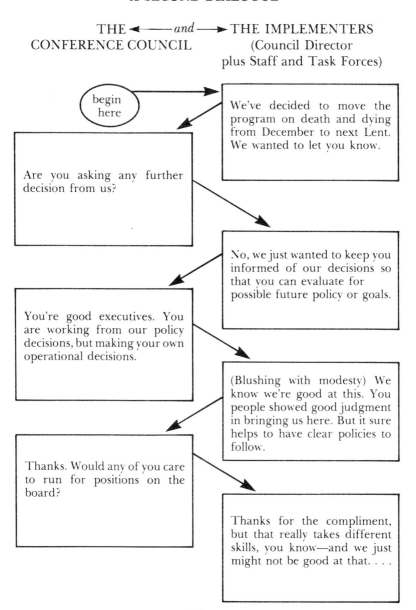

begin here

We've decided to move the program on death and dying from December to next Lent. We wanted to let you know.

Are you asking any further decision from us?

No, we just wanted to keep you informed of our decisions so that you can evaluate for possible future policy or goals.

You're good executives. You are working from our policy decisions, but making your own operational decisions.

(Blushing with modesty) We know we're good at this. You people showed good judgment in bringing us here. But it sure helps to have clear policies to follow.

Thanks. Would any of you care to run for positions on the board?

Thanks for the compliment, but that really takes different skills, you know—and we just might not be good at that. . . .

This team's primary task is to assure the pursuit of goals and objectives set by the Annual Conference and by the board of trust-holders.

The Conference Ministry Team is divided into:

B. *THE PASTORAL MINISTRY TEAM*

The Pastoral Ministry Team consists of the bishop (as general superintendent) and the district superintendents.

These are the persons elected by the conference to lead the pastoral ministry in *their area* of the church.

C. *THE PROGRAM MINISTRY TEAM*

The Program Ministry Team consists of the council director and the staff (the directors of the goal task forces).

It is the body of persons (primarily appointed) who *individually* direct the various programs and support services for the conference. *Collectively,* as a team, they are responsible for healthy interaction among the various ministries, keeping lines of communication and cooperation open, and avoiding unnecessary overlapping.

These three teams are shown graphically in the diagram on page 109.

Perhaps both the *difference* between these teams and the sort of *coordination* required among them could be illustrated by the *difference in their agendas.*

The meeting agenda of the combined Conference Ministry Team should include:
1. Reports and discussions to provide overall monitoring of the health and Spirit of the conference;
2. Proposals and decisions for establishing broad approaches in pursuit of the goals of the conference (the basic strategy);
3. Decisions on *timing*—what needs to be done now, versus later;
4. Decisions on *what to stop doing!*

THE MINISTRY TEAMS

THE CONFERENCE MINISTRY TEAM

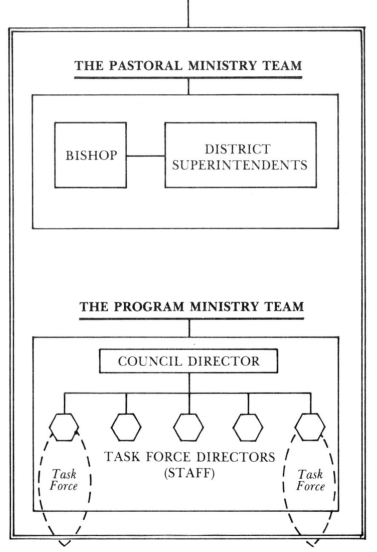

THE PASTORAL MINISTRY TEAM

BISHOP

DISTRICT SUPERINTENDENTS

THE PROGRAM MINISTRY TEAM

COUNCIL DIRECTOR

TASK FORCE DIRECTORS
(STAFF)

Task Force

Task Force

    5. Recommendations to be presented to the conference council and to the Annual Conference for new goals or policies, or revisions of present ones;

    6. Proposals for re-creative activities to keep this team alive and well (*e.g.*, times of prayer or learning together).

The agenda for meetings of the Pastoral Ministry Team should include:

    1. Discussion of matters of pastoral concern, especially for the clergy and clergy families of the conference;

    2. Mutual consultation and support in difficult pastoral situations;

    3. Planning for the rituals and ceremonials of the church;

    4. Planning for the public ministry of the conference in the Church at large and in society.

The agenda for meetings of the Program Ministry Team should include:

    1. Mutual consultation on the design of specific programs to achieve the goals and objectives of the conference;

    2. Planning means for increasing collaboration between goal task forces, and between task forces and support staff functions (secretarial, accounting, etc.);

    3. Planning for development of specific procedures to ensure that all conference program is regularly evaluated, as to both effectiveness and timeliness. While each task force regularly evaluates its own work, the Program Ministry Team provides a framework of principles and procedures to ensure competent, reasonably objective evaluation.

THE STAFF
(Directors of Goal Task Forces)

GOALS AND INTENTIONS OF THE CONFERENCE COME ALIVE ONLY AS THEY ARE TRANSLATED INTO ACTIVITIES THAT WILL PRODUCE THE

DESIRED OUTCOME. (In other words, *goals* are *ends; activities* [program] are *means* to achieve goals.)

Historically, it is very clear that Annual Conferences, Conference Council, and other boards are *best* at articulating the *ends* they desire (call them goals, outcomes, objectives, whatever). It is also very clear that such groups are notoriously *poor* at designing and implementing *means* (programs, activities, tasks). Indeed, it is fair to say that the fundamental health of an Annual Conference or Conference Council is determined partly by the degree to which *it stays out of program design and execution.*

Another axiom is that the design and execution of a program activity is best carried out by *individuals* and *small task forces* of people who are interested and skilled in that specific area.

The council director, as overall program director, should have the responsibility and authority to recruit and employ the staff persons necessary to pursue the goals of the conference vigorously. Indeed, the nature of conference goals, rather than inappropriate conformity to the historic structural patterns of The United Methodist Church, should determine what skilled staff people are needed.

Further, the shape of conference program structures should be affected by the quality of programming at the district and local church levels. As a principle, the lower the level of programming, the better! With *effective programming at local and district levels,* a large conference bureaucracy becomes unneeded and detrimental. When the conference is staffed by goal area, and short-term task forces are set up, a lean and vital conference will result.

Basically, the function of the director of a goal task force is to organize that particular program: to design and implement activities that will forward the mission of the church and achieve the goals and objectives articulated by Annual Conference and by the Conference Council.

Further, the director should carry out regular evaluation of the progress of that particular ministry, with an eye to both improvement of methods and goal/policy implications.

The specific tasks of the directors will vary somewhat, depending on the particular goal to be achieved, but the following would seem to apply to all:

1. Recruit members of the conference with whom the director can work effectively in planning, implementing, and evaluating programs/activities;
2. Coordinate all necessary matters for the successful implementation of the programs/activities planned by his or her goal task force;
3. Coordinate this particular work with the work of the other ministries of the conference (through participation in the Program Ministry Team);
4. Engage in ongoing education and training in the particular specialty in which she or he is serving.

The illustration on page 113 describes the ongoing dialogue between the council director and the directors of the goal task forces.

9. PARTICIPANTS IN THE PROCESS OF MINISTRY

We stated earlier that all Christians are called to ministry in the church. Further, all are called to be both *givers and receivers*. One key form of giving is through *participation in conference and district task forces*. These task forces require the giving of time, of know-how, of special skills necessary to get the job done. Because they exist for a specific purpose and for a specific length of time (they go out of existence automatically unless reassigned), task forces provide an appropriate arena for both ordained and lay ministry.

Other appropriate forms of participation for all Christians are:

THE ONGOING DIALOGUE BETWEEN:

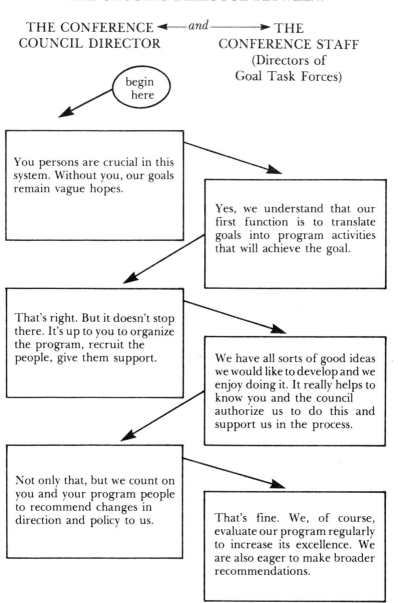

THE CONFERENCE ◄—*and*———► THE
COUNCIL DIRECTOR   CONFERENCE STAFF
                              (Directors of
                              Goal Task Forces)

begin here

You persons are crucial in this system. Without you, our goals remain vague hopes.

Yes, we understand that our first function is to translate goals into program activities that will achieve the goal.

That's right. But it doesn't stop there. It's up to you to organize the program, recruit the people, give them support.

We have all sorts of good ideas we would like to develop and we enjoy doing it. It really helps to know you and the council authorize us to do this and support us in the process.

Not only that, but we count on you and your program people to recommend changes in direction and policy to us.

That's fine. We, of course, evaluate our program regularly to increase its excellence. We are also eager to make broader recommendations.

—taking part in elections
—taking part in major conference events
—making recommendations to conference leaders
—giving money and other resources.

10. But we are RECIPIENTS OF MINISTRY too!

For many of us, it is easier and more acceptable to give than to receive. We are a people full of pride, and often our pride gets in the way of our being open, humble recipients of ministry. As we grow in maturity and understanding, we also grow in our capacity to *receive* and to give thanks!

11. THOSE WHO MIGHT ADVISE

The church, like the human body, is a system. Throughout that system flows the lifeblood of communication, of Spirit, of power.

One of the things we know about systems is that when they are *closed,* they die, and the *more closed* they are, the *faster* they die.

A church that talks and listens only to itself is a closed system. Sooner or later it will die. Obviously, it seems better to be an *open system.* How do we manage this?

First, we maintain an open flow of evaluation and recommendation from all the people of The United Methodist Church.

Second, we seek out and invite the counsel of those from other heritages—wise men and women who see the world from other vantage points than ours. The Conference Council well might recruit a corps of advisors—made up entirely of non-United Methodists.

Third, we open ourselves to the flow of the Holy Spirit in our lives together, through quiet prayer and meditation and through the exuberant wind of shared celebration.

Looking again at the life-flow diagram, we maintain openness by inviting the counsel and input of others early in the "growth" phase.

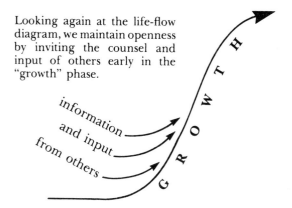

12. BURY THE PROGRAM—HONOR THE PEOPLE

OVER TIME, ALL PROGRAMS AND STRUCTURES DIE. AFTER THEY HAVE PERFORMED THEIR MINISTRY, THEY SHOULD BE LAID TO REST.

All goal task forces—indeed, all structural units—are responsible for proposing their own demise when they perceive that their task is finished. It is also the responsibility of the Conference Ministry Team and the Conference Council, through their ongoing review of

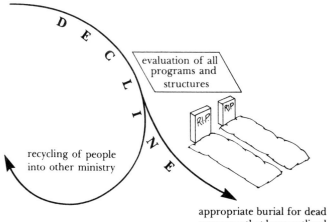

the work of the conference, to say, "It's time to stop." After the regular periodic evaluation, an eliminating procedure should include:

—a ritual of cessation of the program or abolishment of the structural unit—a formal ceremony;

—public celebration of the past ministry performed;

—the freeing of the people and the calling of them to new tasks of ministry.

In other words, BURY THE PROGRAM—HONOR THE PEOPLE!

13. NEXT CYCLE

JUST AS THE LEADERSHIP OF A CONFERENCE MUST PRESIDE OVER THE RITUALS OF BURY-ING THE DEAD AND HONORING THE PEOPLE, SO THEY MUST CALL THE PEOPLE TO NEW LIFE AND ENERGY.

To call the people forth to help them see visions of the church as it could be; to help the conference seek out its clear sense of direction; to help its people live together in peace and joy—this is the work of leadership. John Wesley understood, when he summoned the "people called Methodists" to discuss the mission, to consider ways to carry out ministry, and to talk about living together. The heritage from the Evangelical United Brethren, the Methodist Protestant Church, and all the predecessors of The United Methodist Church provides a rich source for renewed life.

The leadership of the contemporary United Methodist Church must live in constant pulls and tugs—looking to the past, visioning the future, seeking for unity in a church that is never quite sure whether it is a church at all. To reap the richness of past experience and yet to be open to new wisdom—new sources of life outside The United Methodist Church and indeed, outside the Church itself—to all this are our leaders called.

CHAPTER 8

Some Recommendations

Recommendation One

Accept the paradoxical tension in the life of the church. We would like to present some ideas, since this requires a "both and" emphasis—a balance between these primary differences:

Spirit	. . . .	Word
Gift	. . . .	Tradition
Leader	. . . .	Administrator

SPIRIT/WORD AND GIFT/TRADITION

An organization's normal tendency is to become more and more *orderly*—to write down in more and more detail what to do and how to do it. Within bounds, this is fine. But when these details become too burdensome, the processes of innovation and new life are restricted. We would like to see each conference look at its own written material (and the general church look at *The Discipline*), to determine if the proscribed procedures are becoming increasingly *tight*—that is, are they stifling new creative ideas?

LEADER/ADMINISTRATOR

We recommend that training in leadership skills become a normal part of church life. This training should include seminarians, pastors, district superintendents, bishops, council and agency executives, staff, councils, and laymen and -women throughout the church. For example, it might include skills in

—evaluation
—development of alternatives
—decision making
—delegation
—articulation of heritage and vision
—goal setting
—policy development
—chairing of groups.

Recommendation Two

We recommend that a serious study be undertaken of the ways, both common and differing, that women and men participate in the life of The United Methodist Church. As we reported, there was evidence in the study that the usual church pattern tends to give attention to the more traditionally feminine aspects of life (home, children, family, care of the sick and elderly, etc.). The traditionally masculine aspects (work for pay, governmental involvement, finance) receive relatively little attention.

With the changing patterns of women in the work arena—in government, public service; with role reversals—the working wife and the house-husband; with the increase of single women as career professionals, it seems evident that the church must be cognizant of and responsive to these changes.

In addition, our observation of various conference activities indicated that very few lay*men* were present. There is little question that the ordained ministers and laywomen can run the church—they have done so for years!—but we all would be enriched if lay*men* were there, too, in full partnership.

Recommendation Three

Move away from the traditional adversary stance in Annual Conference meetings (and in the various council meetings) by developing skills in *consensual decision making*. This would require the development of new *Rules of Order for United Methodists*, as an alternative to the traditional *Robert's*. Such new rules could honor historic United Methodist values and at the same time increase the effectiveness of the Annual Conference, producing celebration and joy, rather than battle casualties.

Recommendation Four

Develop new policies to promote ongoing renewal for the lives and ministries of the clergy. A fundamental shift away from the "battle" stance—sending out itinerant soldiers with little concern for their welfare—needs consideration.

Of special concern is the tradition that tends to define ministry as "activity"—the more active the better. A revaluing of the ministries of quietness, contemplation, and prayer could produce a new life-rhythm in the church's ordained and unordained ministries—a rhythm of activity and withdrawal modeled on Christ's own ministry.

Recommendation Five

Develop a new theological statement which values the role of the laity in the ongoing ministry of the church. Consider a role shift for clergy, making them primarily the trainers and equippers of the lay ministry—a ministry both to the church and to God's world.

Recommendation Six

Think about the way the informal deification of *large = good* has affected the life of The United Methodist Church. Conferences of several hundred local churches; Annual Conference meetings of over 1000 people; councils with 50 to 200 members—all tend to breed depersonalization and church government by *Robert's Rules*. To be bold, let us consider:

—more and smaller conferences;

—a full-time bishop for each conference;

—procedures for Annual Conference meetings that include workable groups and significant participation, plus the stimulus of great services of worship, preaching, music, and dance;

—Conference Councils small enough (a maximum of 20) that the members really can talk with one another, rather than finding it necessary to function in formal debate modes.

There is much indication in this world that smaller configurations well may add richness to our sometimes impoverished lives. The Church take notice!

Recommendation Seven

The itineracy is in trouble, and it presents the leadership and administration of The United Methodist Church with a crucial test of the validity of the connectional system. The itineracy is under stress as a result of a variety of factors, and clearly some adjustments must be made to deal with the problems that have arisen. The alternatives of muddling through or of exchanging the appointive process for a "call system," with competing congregations and clergy, fail to consider the depth of the crisis and the sources of corporate commitment.

We recommend that both local churches and Annual Conferences address what it means to be covenant community; what is required to enter and live out the commitment to Christ and to one another in congregations and in the conference. Neither laity nor clergy should be allowed to join the church or the conference without in-depth consideration of the commitment they are making and the consequences of being bound to one another in Christian love for the purpose of declaring the good news of Jesus Christ. No amount of authoritarian discipline can effect the voluntary, whole-hearted commitment that is required as lay people join a congregation, or as ministers agree to accept participation in the itineracy. The consultative process can function only when there is genuine commitment to the good of the whole and a willingness to affirm mutual accountability of laity, clergy, superintendents, and bishop. Ways must be found for all to be committed to and accountable to one another.

Recommendation Eight

We must say to our bishops, Be our leaders. By this we mean that we want our bishops
   —to remind us of our great heritage as a people of God;
   —to hold before us visions of God's kingdom on earth and of the special nature of the Church;
   —to call us forth to the tasks of ministry: healing the sick, teaching the young and old, and working for a just and peaceful world.

CHAPTER 9

Conclusion

We have considered in an initial way the contribution to faith and order made by Scripture, tradition, reason, and experience. As a result, we have proposed certain principles and models for leadership and administration, and now we invite you to share your views with us.

1. Recognizing that the contribution of Scripture and tradition to our understanding of faith and order has been explored in a limited fashion, what changes would you make in the analysis, and what additions would you recommend, so that we may more fully understand the contributions of the biblical witness and the history of the church?

2. How do you respond to the analysis of the current situation in regard to leadership and administration? Are the issues and principles valid, in your view? What changes would you make in light of Scripture, tradition, and your own experience?

3. How do you respond to the proposed model for leadership and administration in an Annual Conference? Does it make sense? Is it responsive to Scripture and tradition, as well as to the current experience of the church? Are there modifications you would like to make? Are there other models you would propose?

We invite you to continue the process with us and to invite others to do the same. If it is possible, gather a group of interested people to study the book and reflect together on the issues of faith and order, leadership and administration. We hope this book will be useful in that context, as well.

The principles and models proposed for leadership and administration in The United Methodist Church reflect a continuing search by the Christian community for a corporate life that demonstrates significant unity in the midst of desirable diversity. As chapter 2 indicated, the Pauline and Palestinian expressions of the church were involved in proclaiming the one Lord, Jesus Christ, and in shaping a corporate life that would bear witness to the deep and abiding relationships of those who responded to the gospel. The emphases on Word and tradition on the one hand, and Spirit and gifts on the other, represented the effort to find unity in the faith itself—a unity that would affirm the validity of a variety of expressions and provide the coherence required for their life together. That coherence was sought, not for ease in administration or to facilitate the role of leaders, but to live out in the Christian community the redemptive life made possible through the person and work of Jesus Christ.

Our suggestions for alternative models of leadership and administration are designed not for simple expediency, but to provide ways in which The United Methodist Church might attest to the Lordship of Christ in cogent and coherent ways. The early church did not deny the traditions or contexts in which it was born, nor did it deny the new and deeper life in the Spirit which came. The United Methodist Church cannot deny its roots, nor can it refuse the new gifts and manifestations of the Spirit. The purpose of this book has been to affirm the creative tension between Word and Spirit, office and gift, leadership and administration, and to indicate ways in which we believe The United Methodist Church may demonstrate its unity and diversity in order to uphold its traditions and express the gospel more effectively.

Notes

Chapter 2

1. Hans von Campenhausen, *Ecclesiastical Authority and Spiritual Power* (Stanford, Cal.: Stanford University Press, 1969), p. 294.
2. Adapted from concepts in *Ecclesiastical Authority and Spiritual Power* by Hans von Campenhausen. Used by permission of Stanford University Press.
3. I Corinthians 12:8-10.
4. John Knox, "The Ministry in the Primitive Church," *The Ministry in Historical Perspective*, ed. Richard Niebuhr and Daniel Williams (New York: Harper & Brothers, 1956), p. 13.
5. Hans Küng, *The Church* (New York: Sheed & Ward, 1967), p. 401.
6. von Campenhausen, *Ecclesiastical Authority*, p. 69.
7. *Ibid.*
8. Küng, *Church*, pp. 420-22.
9. Eduard Schweizer, *Church Order in the New Testament* (Naperville, Ill.: Allinson, 1959), p. 84.
10. Cyril Richardson, *Early Christian Fathers* (New York: Macmillan & Co., 1978), p. 75.

Chapter 3

1. James Nelson (Interviewed at United Theological Seminary, Dayton, Ohio, July 17, 1979).
2. John Wesley, *The Works of John Wesley*, ed. Thomas Jackson, 3rd ed. (Grand Rapids: Baker Book House, 1973), 13:248.
3. *Publication of the Wesley Historical Society No. 1 (1896)*, cited by Albert Outler, *John Wesley* (New York: Oxford University Press, 1964), p. 136.
4. Richard Cameron, "The New Church Takes Root," *The History of American Methodism*, ed. Emory S. Bucke (Nashville: Abingdon Press, 1964), 1:115.

5. *Minutes of the Annual Conferences of the Methodist Episcopal Church for the Years 1773–1828,* vol. 1 (New York: T. Mason & G. Lane, 1840).
6. *Works of Wesley,* 13:252.
7. Albert Outler (Interviewed at Perkins Theological Seminary, Dallas, Texas, July 18, 1979).
8. Elden Dale Dunlap, *The System of Itineracy in American Methodism* (Nashville: Board of Higher Education and Ministry of The United Methodist Church), p. 19.
9. Ancel Bassett, *A Concise History of the Methodist Protestant Church* (Pittsburgh: James Robison, 1877), pp. 370-71.
10. Outler, interview.
11. Bruce Behney (Interviewed at United Theological Seminary, Dayton, Ohio, July 25, 1979).
12. Samuel Hough, ed., *Christian Newcomer: His Life, Journal and Achievements* (Dayton, Ohio: Board of Administration, Church of the United Brethren, 1941), p. 48.
13. Carl Eller, *These Evangelical United Brethren* (Dayton, Ohio: Otterbein Press, 1950), p. 34-35.
14. Raymond Albright, *A History of the Evangelical Church* (Harrisburg, Penn.: Evangelical Press, 1945), p. 66.
15. *Ibid.,* p. 41.

Chapter 5

1. Carl Gustav Jung, *Psychological Types* (New York: Harcourt Brace, 1923).

Chapter 6

1. Bion, W. R., *Experiences in Groups* (New York: Basic Books, 1981), p. 63ff.